Praise for the Vision

If you want to play the investment game, you need to know the rules. George Thompson's "Millionaires In Training" is the wealth builder handbook. Study it and play to win!

Lula Ballton
Executive Director, West Angeles Community Development Corp.
Attorney, College Professor, Instructor
Founder & CEO of School Search

George's approach has a power and clarity due to its simplicity and practicality. Put into action his way of shifting us from debt to prosperity is life altering. Out of thousands of highly successful people I coach each year, George is always at the very top and his focus and discipline shows through in everything he teaches. If hard work were like investment capital then George has a portfolio beyond compare. His persistence and dedication are hallmarks of excellence.

Serano Kelly
Chairman and Founder, The Center for Excellence
Author, "The Game"

George has done an absolutely stellar job in making the complicated simple. In this fast moving wealth filled dot com age, we are still struggling with those who do not understand economic divide. It's a breathe of fresh air to finally have a work that will brighten the path and leave instructions for creating and developing economic empowerment for all who would dare to put into action the principles that he has recorded here. You are now holding very valuable keys for economic development, use them wisely and enjoy.

Bishop Donald A. Wright,
D. Min., Ph.D., Jabbok International Fellowship

George has been uniquely blessed and inspired to bring a level of comfort to all who seek to walk in their "power to gain wealth." Millionaires In Training actually inspires you to "attack" wealth. I've seen the lives of many members of my congregation transformed by embracing George's biblical principles combined with his talent. He is an asset to all in the Kingdom. His literary works are a must read!

Bishop Andrew C. Turner, II
Sr. Pastor, New Bethel
Presiding Bishop, Mecca Ministries

This book is an excellent tool in preparing people to embrace principles of wealth and prosperity. Bible-based, it's simple, practical presentation is a must for everyone. Enjoy his strong Christian influences as a fine young man, motivated to educate people in excellence and wealth.

Dr. Wanda A. Turner
Assoc. Pastor. New Bethel
President, The B.E.S.T. CDC

Highly informative . . . reader friendly . . . a must read for the financially ambitious. George Thompson is highly motivated, knowledgeable and ethical.

Deborah Pegues
CFO, West Angeles Church of God In Christ
Author, "Confronting Without Offending"

I've known George Thompson personally for several years. His desire to serve and benefit people is a great strength in these times. George Thompson is one of the great teachers of financial wealth building and practical strategies for success in our day. As you will see in this book, he is clear and practical in his explanation of the finance world's lingo and sometimes confusing strategies. George is a teacher par excellence and compassion. He understands the struggle of the average man or woman, but still encourages us to move higher in our knowledge and wealth building.

Dr. Kenneth Hammonds, BA, M.Div, Ed.D
Personal Success and Leadership Coach
Dir. Of Education, West Angeles COGIC
Founder/Director, School of Success

"Millionaires In Training" provides good insight, with a road map for people who are willing to change their lives and realize financial freedom. The words and examples will penetrate your mind! George Thompson is a professional whom I consider genuine, positive and dedicated to making a difference in the lives of people he encounters. He is energetic, intelligent and possesses a rare gift.. .and that is "helping people help themselves"

Charles Williams
General Manager US Cellular
Board Member, American Red Cross
Board Member, Big Brother/Sister

George's valuable techniques to sound financial planning make this, (Millionaires In Training seminar), one of our most popular classes. He shows everyone how using their M.I.N.D. can achieve our financial goals and become Millionaires in Training.

Mark Tallman
Dir. of Training, Penske College
Penske Automotive Group

This book offers a step-by-step guide to eliminate debt and accumulate wealth. It uses clear examples, worktables and direct language to simplify the process. George is an enthusiastic and charismatic professional who delivers a powerful and pertinent message.

Sonia Alvarado
Producer, "Making It! Minority Success Stories"
Emmy Award Winning small business television show

In the face of what may seem like an unattainable path for the average individual, the road to true financial security, George is the investor's equivalent to the pied piper. Not only does George show us how to get there he plays a great tune along the way.

John W. Patton, Esq.
Partner, PASTERNAK, PASTERNAK & PATTON
Fmr. President Beverly Hills Bar

I found the book to be of great value, especially the section on Debt Elimination. I needed to have a plan and the book outline provides excellent examples for those willing to be free from debt. George's seminars are very thought provoking and he challenges the participants to begin thinking about becoming a Millionaire.

Delaphine Prysock
Assistant Dean of Students/Director of Housing
Whittier College

As the Silicone Valley continues to produce 65 millionaires per day, smart young investment advisor, George Thompson has taken on the challenge of ensuring that this New Economy leaves no one out. Millionaires In Training is an extremely well written resource on the ABC's of investing. Readers who heed its principles can be active participants in the greatest economic boom in history.

This significant book paves the way for us to see scores of budding millionaires where few existed before. Congratulations to George for helping to literally turn consumers into investors!

Joseph Loeb
Founder and CEO, Break Away Technologies

Recently, having the privilege of meeting George and sitting under his tutoring, I was immensely convinced that he was an apostle of finance with a voice of pristine clarity on the subject. His integrity, sincerity, and particularly his genuine love for God along with his determination to see God's people prosper, stood as giants in his field of success. His uncanny ability to reduce profound things to simplicity and convert information to impartation makes him more than an expert on the subject, but a master teacher and an anointed man of God. The wise would take heed to the instructions of George B. Thompson.

Carl C. Alexander, Bishop
Tabernacle of Praise, New York

When I first met George Thompson. I was heavily in debt. I wanted to become debt free and desired to buy a home, but I did not know where to start. The information that he provided in his seminar and in his book helped me to pay off 75% of my outstanding debt and shortly after, I was able to purchase a home. George's seminars and book helped me to think wealth.

Shirley Hall
Forestville, Maryland

Reading "Millionaires In Training" is your first step to achieving financial security. The second step, however, is the key to achieving; you must implement this game plan to gain your goal of financial freedom.

Joseph G. Devanney, C.L.U.
Professor, UCLA

MILLIONAIRES
IN
TRAINING

MILLIONAIRES
IN
TRAINING
THE WEALTH BUILDER

George B. Thompson

Prosperity Publishing
CALIFORNIA

Millionaires In Training
©2003, George B. Thompson

ISBN: 0-9674858-3-5

Printed in the United States of America

Cover created by Larry Levy—Drawing Board Studios, dbstudios171@cs.com

George Thompson is available as a keynote speaker at conventions, seminars, and workshops as well as for organizations wishing to share how anyone can become a "Millionaire in Training." If you would like to discuss a possible speaking engagement or obtain additional copies of the book, he can be reached at:

Trainingmillionaires.com

Millionaires In Training
P.O. Box 90761
Los Angeles, CA 90009

Thompsongb@aol.com
or
(800) 452-8001

Dedication

I would like to dedicate this book to all who wish
to take the next step toward financial freedom.

To anyone who is ready to move to the next level.

To those who stand up one more time after being knocked down.

And to those who are willing to accept guidance through my sincere efforts.

Acknowledgements

I am very fortunate to have so many people to thank. The following list is by no means complete. First, I will start with God because He makes all things possible. Next, I would like to thank the greatest parents in the world, George B. Thompson, Sr. and Morsie L. Thompson. They have always loved and supported me even in my craziest endeavors. Without a doubt the greatest twin-sister in the world, Jenifer, who is always there for me; and my older bother, Darrell, from whom I have learned many life lessons.

I also would like to thank Bishop Charles E. Blake, pastor of my church, West Angeles Church of God in Christ. Special thanks also to the Director of Christian Education for allowing me to teach a class on finances, Dr. Kenneth Hammonds whose encouragement has been invaluable.

To all the people who made this project possible thank you first to my editors, proofreaders and temperature checkers: Kimberley Ingram, Dellareasa Woodert, Darnell and Deborah Pegues, Alicia Cole, LaTonya Pegues, and Sunshine Njeri. Then to Todd "EJ" Douphner whose creativity has taken this project to another level.

People at work who have contributed to the success of my efforts are my Branch Manager, Tony (TD) Didonato, who has been completely supportive of me, Phil Waxelbaum, for giving me a job and pushing me towards excellence. Also to Charles Gaskin, Rev. Audrey Gaskin, Deborah Sakol and Steve Camp.

Thank you to Joe Brozic of Goal Getters for not only his encouragement but his excellent consulting skills.

Thank you also to The Center for Excellence, Serano Kelly and all my partners that keep me "in the ZONE!"

I also would like to thank Andre Burman from MFS who sent me the hypothetical illustration, and Nick Willett from Alliance for always supporting me.

Most importantly, I would like to thank all the thousands of people that have allowed me to share my vision for making millionaires. Without your feedback and questions, this book would not be possible. If you see anything that could be improved upon, please write, email, or phone me. Remember, this book is for **YOU.**

Table of Contents

Chapter VI:

Introduction

Amid the pending globalization of unified financial practices, the increasing cyber access to banking and the current economic expansion, it is crucial for those with an eye on the future to take a stronger foothold on today's economic growth. As such, it has been an aspiration of mine to ensure availability of financial wherewithal to those that would not otherwise have access. Regardless of any existing financial status, I believe that anyone can become a *millionaire in training* if they can grasp the beneficial principles, which I've outlined in basic terms.

Several years ago, I recognized the disproportionate distribution of wealth in our country and its ever-widening gap. It troubled me to think that the general populace did not benefit from the financially viable economy enjoyed by a select few. It is commonly accepted that the poor will be with us always, however, the incredulous statistics are astounding. I wondered why, without an established caste system, did so few move from meager existence to affluence. How were these fortunes amassed? What basic factors created an environment of prosperity? What was it that caused those who acquired wealth quickly to lose fortunes within months? What characteristics facilitated the preservation of wealth? To unmask the mystery of this dilemma, I began to study how those individuals whose implausible wealth was obtained and more importantly maintained.

My many years of study yielded several interesting facts. The most outstanding factor is the astonishing tradition in our society to establish generations of debtors. We owe everyone. There are even bumper stickers that say "I owe. . . I owe . . . so off to work I go". It is an expected phenomenon. So accepted is this tradition that one can barely exist without a 'credit history,' which is the "politically correct" way to say an established record of debt. Debt transcends class, race and sex. Debt knows no bounds. Rather than probe into the psychological causes, or the unfortunate circumstances that cause an overwhelming obligatory existence, I thought it more appropriate to examine the solution to this sad predicament.

Once relieved of the burdens associated with debt, the most logical course of action seemed to be the accumulation of wealth. In proceeding with my particular investigation, I learned that not all millionaires obtained wealth in an underhanded manner. I also learned that most millionaires lived a life void of impulsive spending. But the most substantial fact about millionaires is their ability to take ownership of their future. During severe times, they seem to thrive rather than withdraw because of their moneymaking intelligence, and unwavering discipline. They are not controlled by popular opinion. They do not act out of fear nor do they react to trends or fads. They remain focused.

Unfortunately, the lives of too many are dictated by debt. They do not control their own destiny. Most individuals live deeply in debt and are creating more along the way. I saw it as spending his or her future; no one wanted to practice delayed gratification. When most people want to make a purchase, they must first ask "Massa Card"; and when they travel, they have to get their "Visa"; and if there is a desire to experience dining at its best, no one could leave home without "it".

As a result of my fact finding, I determined that these basic principles must be shared with the masses to encourage economic growth. Most people believe the financial world is a highly evolved and difficult field of study when in fact, it is not. But there was no one that I knew of who wanted to take the time to relay this information to those most in need. So, I took it upon myself to outline fundamental principles in a language that anyone could comprehend. I began to donate my time by teaching classes at the beginner level. I found that most people were generally eager to learn about finances and how to accumulate wealth. The class, *Millionaires In Training,* began to change the lives of many people. The feedback I received was so encouraging; it began to enhance the quality of my own life. Students from the class could retire two years earlier, send their children to college, or live free from debt. The more I observed phenomenal change the greater my sense of commitment to help people create and grow wealth.

The result is this book, a product of my intense preparation, planning and execution with the objective to help others receive financial independence. I hope this book will teach principles, encourage discipline, and produce future millionaires!

Chapter

I

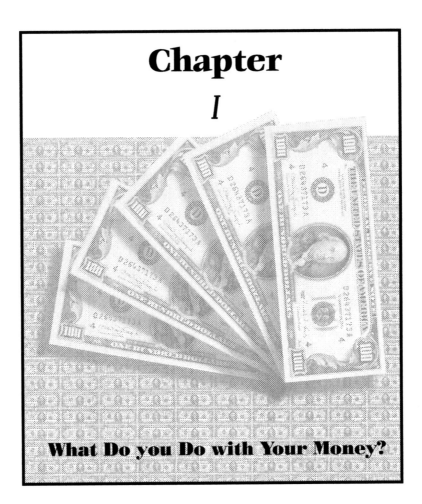

What Do you Do with Your Money?

THERE ARE THREE THINGS YOU CAN DO WITH YOUR MONEY:

Spend it, many of us are experts at that;

Lend it, which is to put it in a bank, or purchase bonds;

Own something, which is our ultimate goal.

This book is about **Ownership.** Your money should be working as hard as you do to obtain ownership. Ownership paves the way to becoming a millionaire. There are four attributes necessary in becoming a millionaire: 1) Money, 2) Intelligence, 3) Need, and 4) Discipline.

Millionaire in training

YOU NEED ONLY TO USE YOUR M.I.N.D.

MONEY
You have heard the phrase "it takes money to make money". This is essentially true. The problem is not that you don't have money, but rather you are not using your money wisely. For example, the money you spend on credit card debt or on leasing expensive cars could be put to far better use.

INTELLIGENCE
You need to use your intelligence when it comes to spending money. You should funnel your money in a manner that is conducive to being financially successful. The 'get rich quick' scheme, the lottery ticket, or the Vegas Jackpot will not produce financial freedom. Statistics indicate that the average person loses more money on a quest for the get rich quick scheme. In fact, the odds are against people who think they can make money playing the lottery or gambling. Mathematicians who study odds say that they calculate that a lottery player would have to spend $200,000 over time to accrue $100,000 in winnings. That could explain why some of the names of multiple lottery winners can be found in U.S. Bankruptcy Court records, on lists of delinquent taxpayers and as defendants in debt collection lawsuits. Having financial intelligence requires doing what we can, with the resources that we have, to maintain optimum results.

NEED

Your need to be financially secure must be stronger than any other desire. With that strong, passionate need to obtain financial freedom, you will overlook the "wants" that have controlled you in the past. You will no longer "want" to impress people with things you cannot afford. You will stop investing in things that depreciate in value, all because your need for financial freedom will cause you to become more focused. Wealth building, college funding, starting a business, retirement, or some other financial goal will be more important than spending.

DISCIPLINE

Discipline is one of the most crucial aspects of achieving greatness and securing financial freedom. There is no exception. The one quality that is present in all people who have achieved financial success is their ability to remain disciplined. This unwavering discipline will cause you to stay focused during difficult times. Discipline will stop you from increasing your debt while causing you to decrease your frivolous spending. You will become a 'Wealth Builder'.

WHERE DOES YOUR MONEY GO?

LIVING AT YOUR MEANS

Your "means" is the mechanism by which you maintain a living. That is to say, the substance that supports your lifestyle. It is generally accepted that most Americans live above their "means". As an illustration, we will compare two neighbors who have parallel incomes. Mil N. Aire and Don N. Debt both work as salesmen. Totaling their salary and commissions, they each make $75,000 a year. Don is determined to live better than his neighbor and as a result he has added two new rooms to his home, he owns a luxury vehicle and an SUV, he has put a pool in his backyard and he is planning a trip to Europe in the summer. His suits are custom made, his wife is looking for her third fur coat, and his young children have the best designer clothes money can buy. Unfortunately, his yearly income of $75,000 does not support such an extravagant lifestyle. Don has hit the maximum limit on all of his credit cards, he has taken a second mortgage out on his home, he has borrowed thousands from his wife's family and his bank loans exceed $10,000.

His neighbor, Mil, is content with his home in its original state. Mil uses his commission checks for his investment portfolio. On top of contributing the maximum to his 401k plan, Mil saves a total of 25% of his gross income. Mil has paid off his two vehicles and pays cash for any of his purchases. Mil and his family are flying to a summer resort and he has purchased his tickets using the frequent flyer miles he accumulated through his sales travels. Mil's wife has a home based business and the additional funds generated are used to-

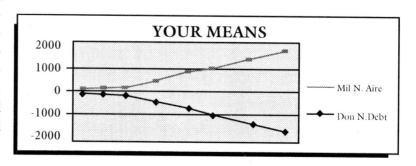

wards their children's college fund. The Aires have decided to live on one paycheck. Mil has saved 6 months of his salary for an emergency.

As you can see, the net worth of each family is drastically different. Mil's worth continues to climb steadily as indicated by the graph on page 4. His investments are growing, his savings are increasing, and his future is becoming more and more secure.

Don, on the other hand, continues to sink deeper into debt. He must continue to borrow money to maintain his lifestyle which is consistently above his means. His lifestyle far exceeds the actual amount he takes home and in order to maintain it he must find additional means. He has not considered getting a second job; consequently he proceeds to search for other ways to gain a means to match his voracious spending.

Many people believe that if they had more money they would not be in debt. As you can see from the two neighbors, the amount of money does not determine your net worth. It is the manner in which the income is used that is the determining factor. What you do with your money is more important than how much money you have.

As shown in this illustration, we must learn to live **beneath** our means and not above or even at our means. Some people spend more than what they make (above their means); and some people spend every penny they bring home (at their means); but as Millionaires-In-Training, we must spend less than what we make and reserve a portion for the future.

One of the biggest misconceptions held by most people is equating success with living at their means. They don't understand if you are living at your means, spending every penny, you are actually living above your means. Primarily, you need to save a minimum of 10% of your income. If you do not, you are living above your means. If you say you cannot afford to save, there is a list of convincing points of action at the end of this chapter that will assist you in saving 10% of your income. It is important to understand that saving money is not an option. If you do not save a portion of your income, you will be paying at least that and more in interest payments to a credit card company. Let us look at the financial escapades of Don N. Debt.

The previous illustration depicts how people stay in debt. First, they don't save 10% of their income. An individual should essentially save the equivalent of 3 to 6 months of their salary. The 3 to 6 months variable is dependent upon the situation. If you are married with 2 base salaries and no children, then 3 months' savings would be sufficient. However, if you have a family and one income, 6 months' savings would be the minimum. It is essential that you retain an emergency fund because things will always come up and you don't want to depend upon credit cards (spending future earnings).

Our pal Don did not have a savings plan to rely upon. If any crisis occurred, he would fall deeper into debt. How about this scenario; if he had a family emergency, someone died and he had to fly to the funeral. Then his sister got married and he had to buy gifts. Subsequently, his car broke down and he had to have it fixed. Soon afterward, he needed to have his roof

repaired. There is no reprieve for Don N. Debt. His financial dilemma could not support these or any foreseeable expenses like holidays, costs associated with his job, or the probability of unexpected illnesses and accidents. The answer to his quandary is resourceful planning for those rainy days because later he will find that debt is expensive. An

MONEY IN MOTION

Installment Debt	Budget	Prosperity Dollars
Major Credit Card 1	Mortgage/Rent Payment	Savings
Major Credit Card 2	Cable	401K
Department Store Card 1	Utilities	403b TSA
Department Store Card 2	Telephone	Brokerage Account
Car Loan	Food/groceries/eating out	Education
Student Loan	Entertainment	Home Equity

individual can take the spiral into the vast abyss of debt (anti-millionaire) with little hope of getting out or an individual can use their M.I.N.D. and whirl into prosperity as you take another step towards becoming a Millionaire-In-Training.

The object of this exercise is to find out where your money goes. This may be one of the most startling exercises you've ever completed. If you are spending large amounts of money in installment debt, if your budget exceeds your income, or if you have little or nothing to put into the prosperity column, you will always be an anti-millionaire.

An anti-millionaire makes other people rich. Ideally, you want to have more money in the prosperity column and nothing in installment debt, which will start you on your way to becoming a millionaire. Our goal is to take all of the money out of installment debt and put it into prosperity dollars. Instead of making other people wealthy, you will become wealthy yourself. Let us get started.

MONEY IN MOTION

INSTALLMENT DEBT	BUDGET	PROSPERITY DOLLARS

DEBT ELIMINATOR

Name of Debt	Minimum Monthly	Total Debt	Debt Eliminator	Priority	Time
Dept. Store Credit Card #1		$ 275			
Dept. Store Credit Card #2		$ 500			
Dept. Store Credit Card #3		$ 1,200			
Major Credit Card #1		$ 1,500			
Major Credit Card #2		$ 3,000			
Major Credit Card #3		$ 4,200			
Automobile		$ 11,000			
Student Loan		$ 20,000			
Mortgage		$ 130,000			

Table I-1

This step will take you from anti-millionaire status towards the coveted position of financial freedom. Input your financial information into the graph at the end of this chapter (table I–6), starting with a list of your creditors and the outstanding debt owed.

The next step is to list the minimum monthly amount required on each debt. What you are ultimately going to do is pay the minimum amount required with the exception of one. This debt will be your number one priority. So, let us list your debt in order of priority. I like to start with the lowest outstanding balance and work upward from there. Please note, the figures in our sample are rounded off for simplicity's sake; however, please be accurate in your account to reflect a more precise financial representation.

DEBT ELIMINATOR

Name of Debt	Minimum Monthly Payment	Total Debt	Debt Eliminator	Priority	Time
Dept. Store Credit Card #1	$ 15	$ 275		1	
Dept. Store Credit Card #2	$ 25	$ 500		2	
Dept. Store Credit Card #3	$ 40	$ 1,200		3	
Major Credit Card #1	$ 45	$ 1,500		4	
Major Credit Card #2	$ 90	$ 3,000		5	
Major Credit Card #3	$ 125	$ 4,200		6	
Automobile	$ 275	$ 11,000		7	
Student Loan	$ 250	$ 20,000		8	
Mortgage	$ 1,200	$ 130,000		9	

Table I-2

Your situation may not be as drastic, however there are others who are experiencing a more severe financial picture. Do not become dazed by your current situation; it *is* possible to climb out of financial despair.

Table I-2 reflects a monthly debt payment of 2,065.00. Which means if this person paid all of their bills on time each month; their debt payment would be over 2,000.00.

This does not include utilities, clothing, food, and certainly not an entertainment allowance.

THIS PERSON IS A SLAVE TO THEIR DEBT

THERE ARE FIVE CHARACTERISTICS OF DEBT SLAVERY:

1. You are making someone else rich from the sweat of your brow.
2. You have a feeling that you will always be paying off debts.
3. You have low financial intellect; financial freedom eludes you because you are not aware of the alternatives.
4. You are in bondage because you have no money and can not do what you want.
5. You have worked all your life and have nothing to show for it.

Let me put it to you this way. If you were working somewhere and your boss told you that he could not afford to pay you any more, but he had worked out an equivalent plan for you that went like this: He had obtained a little apartment above the business, where you and your family could stay. He would give you a beat up little car and provide you with just enough gas to pick up your kids from school; and if the car breaks down, you have to work overtime to fix it. If there is a sale at the local department store, he will pick up a few sale items for you. If you live on this type of equivalent plan, guess what? You are a slave.

I know this sounds harsh and even painful to accept; but only you can get rid of the pain. You have to make some changes. Let me ask you a question. If one of your closest relatives became sick or died, do you have enough money today to leave town and visit them, or do you have to ask a credit card for permission?

DEBT ELIMINATOR

Name of Debt	Minimum Monthly Payment	Total Debt	Debt Eliminator	Priority	Time
Dept. Store Credit Card #1	$ 15	$ 275	$ 115	1	3 Months
Dept. Store Credit Card #2	$ 25	$ 500		2	
Dept. Store Credit Card #3	$ 40	$ 1,200		3	
Major Credit Card #1	$ 45	$ 1,500		4	
Major Credit Card #2	$ 90	$ 3,000		5	
Major Credit Card #3	$ 125	$ 4,200		6	
Automobile	$ 275	$ 11,000		7	
Student Loan	$ 250	$ 20,000		8	
Mortgage	$ 1,200	$ 130,000		9	

Table I-3

The next step is to pay more than the monthly amount. Ideally, $100 over the minimum amount is suggested. The minimum monthly amount due on priority #1 is $15. If $115 is paid to department store credit card #2, it will take approximately 3 months to pay this account in full. This timeframe includes the approximate interest payments as well.

It feels good after reaching that first accomplishment. Two things are extremely important during this initial stage. 1) Make sure you keep up with your other minimum payments and; 2) do not (and this is very important), incur any additional debt. Here is where your NEED and DISCIPLINE are required. Your NEED to be debt free must be so powerful that you will DISCIPLINE yourself to do without the 'frills' of life. If you don't, you will be weighted down by debt all of your life.

In the fourth month you will have an excess of $115 because your priority #1 is now paid. What do you do with that $115? No, the answer is not to celebrate with a $100 dinner. You apply this surplus to priority #2.

After 3 months of steady minimum payments, priority #2 has now been reduced approximately to $350. In the 4th month you add your $115 surplus to the $25 minimum payment and you pay $140 per month on priority #2. This will reduce priority #2 to $0 in 3 months. Calculating from the starting point, priority #2 will be paid in full in 6 months. After priority #2 is paid you apply $140 to priority #3 and so on.

DEBT ELIMINATOR

Name of Debt	Minimum Monthly Payment	Total Debt	Debt Eliminator	Priority	Time
Dept. Store Credit Card #1	$ 15	$ 275	$ 115	1	3 Months
Dept. Store Credit Card #2	$ 25	$ 500	$ 140	2	6 Months
Dept. Store Credit Card #3	$ 40	$ 1,200	$ 180	3	12 Months
Major Credit Card #1	$ 45	$ 1,500	$ 225	4	17 Months
Major Credit Card #2	$ 90	$ 3,000	*$ 315	5	22 Months
Major Credit Card #3	$ 125	$ 4,200	**$ 440	6	26 Months
Automobile	$ 275	$ 11,000	$ 715	7	33 Months
Student Loan	$ 250	$ 20,000	$ 965	8	83 Months
Mortgage	$ 1,200	$ 130,000	$ 2,165	9	81 Months
Total	$ 2,065	$ 171,675	$ 2,165		108 Months

Table I-4

Following this formula, the table below reflects the reduction of all debt to a zero balance and the approximate time required to reach this goal. This is known as a debt multiplier. The debt multiplier becomes the debt eliminator.

DEBT ELIMINATOR

Name of Debt	Starting Bal. Amt. Due:/Monthly Payment	Month 3 Amt. Due:/Monthly Payment	Month 6 Amt. Due:/Monthly Payment	Month 10 Amt. Due:/Monthly Payment	Month 12 Amt. Due:/Monthly Payment	Month 18 Amt. Due:/Monthly Payment	Month 26 Amt. Due:/Monthly Payment	Month 45 Amt. Due:/Monthly Payment	Month 81 Amt. Due:/Monthly Payment
Dept. Store Credit Card #2	$275/ $115	$0	$0	$0	$0	$0	$0	$0	$0
Dept. Store Credit Card #1	$500/ $25	$425/ $140	$0	$0	$0	$0	$0	$0	$0
Dept. Store Credit Card #3	$1,200/ $40	$1080/ $40	$960/ $180	$240/ $180	$0	$0	$0	$0	$0
Major Credit Card #1	$1500/ $45	$1365/ $45	$1230/ $45	$1050/ $45	$960/ $225	$0	$0	$0	$0
Major Credit Card #2	$3000/ $90	$2730/ $90	$2460/ $90	$2100/ $90	$1920/ $90	$1115/ $250	$0	$0	$0
Major Credit Card #3	$4200/ $125	$3825/ $125	$3450/ $125	$2950/ $125	$2075/ $850	$0	$0	$0	$0
Automobile	$11,000/ $275	$10,175/ $275	$9350/ $275	$8250/ $275	$7700/ $275	$6050/ $275	$3850/ $715	$0	$0
Student Loan	$20,000/ $250	$19,250/ $250	$18,500/ $250	$17,500/ $250	$17,000/ $250	$15,500/ $250	$13,500/ $250	$0	$0
Mortgage	$130,000/ $1200	$126,400/ $1200	$122,800/ $1200	$118,000/ $1200	$115,600/ $1200	$108,400/ $1200	$98,800/ $1200	$76,000/ $2165	$0

Table I-5

As you can see, using this structured *Debt Multiplier*, you can conceivably pay off over $171,000, including a home, in less than 9 years. The most incredible part is that you are using only $100.00 more than the minimum payment.

Of course, there are variables, which might include missed payments because of emergencies, credit card interest, etc. However, if you train yourself to focus on the end result, you can achieve this significant objective. The advantage of this plan is the additional $2,200 you will have upon completing the Debt Eliminator.

The common mistake people make is believing that they don't have enough money. This is usually not the case. They have enough money; unfortunately, it is not being utilized correctly. Don N. Debt earned an ample amount of money. He simply did not understand that it cost more money to be in debt than it does to be rich. When I speak with people, invariably they tell me they cannot afford to invest. My response to that is, they already are. They are investing in debt.

Being in debt is a very expensive investment. For example, if you have $5,000 on a credit card and $5,000 in a mutual fund, and you pay $100 a month on both the credit card and the mutual fund. The interest rate for the credit card is 10% (I am being generous here); and the rate of return for the mutual fund is10%.

It will take you a little under 5 ½ years or 64 months to pay off the loan, that is if you continue to pay $100 and don't drop to the minimum payment routine. You will pay $1,492.00 in interest, which brings you to a grand total of $6,492.

Most people think the interest is the only cost that you incur. This is not true! You incur opportunity costs as well. That same $5,000 invested in a mutual fund, with a 10% compounded annual return over that same 64 month period, will grow to $16,834.42.

I use this illustration to show how, after 5 years, one person has over $16,000 and another has zero. If you only set a goal to get out of debt, you will be setting a goal to get to zero. You are not a zero, you are a Millionaire; however, you are in training. Realistically, if someone was paying 19.5% interest on a credit card, it would take them 8½ years or 102.5 months to pay off the debt. That person will have paid a total of $10,380.00. This is more than twice what was charged. Take that same amount and put it in a mutual fund at 10% compounded annually over the same period of time and it could gross $27,462.19.

It does not take a genius to see that you can do more with $27,000 than you can with zero. Consequently, it cost more money to be in debt than it does to be rich. It takes a 40% return in the stock market to break even with debt if you are in the 28% federal tax bracket and pay 12% interest. This calculation does not include state taxes, which increases your requirement just to break even with debt. Every person is an investor. I would rather see you invest in assets that appreciate or are conducive to you building wealth than investing in entities that make other people rich. I would like to show one last example of higher debt with a $500.00 debt multiplier (see Table 1–7).

It is now time to eliminate your debt. Complete the graph using your financial information. Do not leave anything out. You need a realistic picture of where you stand on the net worth meter.

DEBT ELIMINATOR

Name of Debt	Minimum Monthly Payment	Total Debt	Debt Eliminator	Priority	Time

Table 1-6

DEBT ELIMINATOR

Name of Debt	Minimum Monthly Payment	Total Debt	Debt Eliminator	Priority	Time
Dept. Store Credit Card #1	$ 15	$ 275	$ 515	1	1 Months
Dept. Store Credit Card #2	$ 25	$ 500	$ 540	2	2 Months
Dept. Store Credit Card #3	$ 40	$ 1,200	$ 580	3	4 Months
Major Credit Card #1	$ 45	$ 1,500	$ 625	4	6 Months
Major Credit Card #2	$ 150	$ 5,000	$ 775	5	12 Months
Major Credit Card #3	$ 210	$ 7,000	$ 985	6	17 Months
Automobile	$ 610	$ 28,000	$ 1,595	7	28 Months
2nd Mortgage	$ 300	$ 30,000	$ 1,895	8	44 Months
Mortgage	$ 1,700	$ 230,000	$ 3,595	9	87 Months
Total	$ 3,095	$ 303,475	$ 11,105		201 Months

Table I-7

Chapter

II

100 Ways To Save

Or Running The Savings Maze

Now that we have a clear idea of how and when we will get out of debt, I will show you 100 ways to save money. These tips will do away with many habits that are contrary to producing wealth. Come, let's run the savings maze!

1
Take care of what you already have!

7
When using a cellular telephone, do not accept incoming calls. This cuts down on small talk and avoids paying for wrong numbers or sales calls.

6
If you cannot gain control over your need to talk long distance, purchase a phone card. Imagine if you have to go to the store and pay cash in advance for 100 minutes, you will have a tendency to stop wasting time on the telephone. You would stop using the phone out of boredom; you are on the clock.

2
Do not take advice from anyone more messed up than you.

3
When possible, refinance your home, then use the surplus money to pay down debt. Then pay off the house. Think Big! Do not just pay off installment debt, pay off all debt.

5
Talk is cheap! Reduce your telephone bill by changing to an inexpensive carrier. Whenever possible, use the Internet. It is less expensive to send e-mail to your friends and family. However, if you must communicate verbally, call at off-peak hours. Write down what you want to talk about before you call. Hang up when you have said what is on your list. Block 900 numbers and don't accept collect calls.

4
If you must operate on credit, call your creditors to negotiate a lower interest rate or switch to a credit card that already has a comparatively low rate. REMEMBER a credit card is not a solution, just a Band-Aid.

8
Cancel all unnecessary calling features on your phone. Why pay monthly for a feature you only use twice a year?

9
Do not buy penny stocks. Famous last words, "This company is coming out with a product that is going to revolutionize the world as we now know it." Please suppress the lottery mentality.

10
Avoid buying things on sale *just* because they are on sale. There is nothing wrong with getting great deals. However, some people have closets or pantries full of stuff they do not use. But they always say, "It was 50% off and I couldn't pass it up." Well save 100% and don't buy it!

11
Do not leave every light on when you are home. If you had to put a dime in the light switch to turn on the lights or a quarter to watch TV you would be more careful with how you used your utilities.

12
Unplug the extra refrigerator. You would be amazed how much electricity you can save.

13
Adjust your thermostat when you are away from home for long periods of time. My mother used to say, "Don't heat up the furniture." (I grew up in Minnesota). The same holds true for your air conditioner. Do not pay to keep the walls cool.

14
Purchase a used car. New cars have higher monthly payments, and the car itself decreases in value. Used car purchases also save on insurance premiums. You get lower rates on used cars.

19
Routine upkeep on your vehicle will save you lump sums of money when the car breaks down from lack of maintenance.

21
Change your oil regularly. Oil in a car is like blood in a human. It is vital to operating efficiently.

20
Avoid putting high-octane fuel in your vehicle. For example, 87 rather than 92 premium does not offer much difference.

22
When leasing a car, find out what the purchase price is and save the difference.

18
Drive your car carefully. It will keep you from paying outrageous amounts on speeding tickets and increase the longevity of your brakes.

17
Rather than spending money on costly car insurance premiums, spend extra time searching out the most economical insurance rate.

16
When purchasing a new car, buy a car at the end of the year or at the very least, at the end of the month. The sales staff will give you a better deal so they can make their monthly quota.

15
If you purchase a new car, pay off the car loan and keep the car for several years. The money you previously used to pay your car note can now be used to invest in building wealth. Forget about keeping up with the Joneses, they are not Millionaires.

28
Avoid holiday impulse buying. If you wait to purchase gifts right before a holiday, the tendency is to spend more and bargain shop less because of the time constraint. Budget your money during the year and only spend what you have budgeted.

29
Take advantage of your employee benefits plans. Most people are not aware of the benefits provided. Subscriptions, optical examinations, glasses, etc.

27
Do not wait until the Christmas season to buy Christmas presents. Purchase Christmas presents all year round. In fact, the biggest shopping day should be a few days after Christmas. Most items are reduced 70%.

23
We already know the effects that smoking has on the body. However, from a financial standpoint, consider the cost to keep up such a habit. The cost of the cigarette packs, the cost incurred to clean your clothes, your dental bills, etc. The cost averages approximately $2,500.00 each year.

26
Avoid paying full price for designer clothes. You can shop at outlet stores, or purchase your clothes during the off season, or shop during "end of the season" sales.

25
Do not buy designer clothes for babies. This boosts *your* self-esteem, not the baby's. A two-year-old is not aware of the latest fashion trends.

24
Do not buy Life Insurance for children. When a child dies, the principal loss is emotional. Insurance is to indemnify (reimburse) you for a financial loss. Children do not normally contribute substantial income to the household. Therefore, the monthly premiums on life insurance for children could be better used elsewhere.

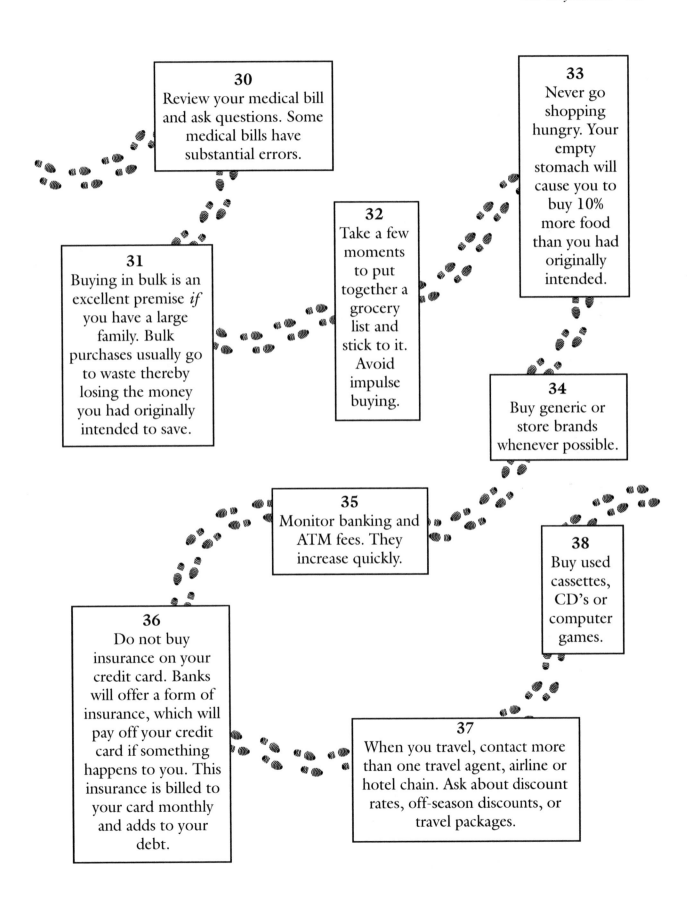

30
Review your medical bill and ask questions. Some medical bills have substantial errors.

31
Buying in bulk is an excellent premise *if* you have a large family. Bulk purchases usually go to waste thereby losing the money you had originally intended to save.

32
Take a few moments to put together a grocery list and stick to it. Avoid impulse buying.

33
Never go shopping hungry. Your empty stomach will cause you to buy 10% more food than you had originally intended.

34
Buy generic or store brands whenever possible.

35
Monitor banking and ATM fees. They increase quickly.

36
Do not buy insurance on your credit card. Banks will offer a form of insurance, which will pay off your credit card if something happens to you. This insurance is billed to your card monthly and adds to your debt.

37
When you travel, contact more than one travel agent, airline or hotel chain. Ask about discount rates, off-season discounts, or travel packages.

38
Buy used cassettes, CD's or computer games.

40
Lottery tickets seem like a minimal purchase. However, an individual could spend hundreds of dollars on lottery tickets each year and only recoupe a $5.00 win. Look at the chances of your winning versus the money spent. Risk v. reward. You actually have two chances of winning, 'slim and none'!

41
Bring your lunch and snacks to work. Ten dollars a day multiplied by 5 times per week is $50. Multiply that by 52 weeks a year and you will have spent $2600 a year.

42
Invest in 401k retirement plans or IRA. You use pretax dollars for these plans. This is money you will not have to pay to your least favorite relative, Uncle Sam.

39
Cancel subscriptions to magazines. Buy your favorite magazines monthly only when you are sure that you have the time to read them. There are months when you do not have time to read magazines and you accumulate many unread magazines.

43
Get a second job. That job should be a 'Debt Job'. A job whose income will be used solely to pay off debt. Example: answering service, kiddie chauffeur, dog, plant or house sitter, cleaning service, personal shopper, etc.

44
Utilize your Debt Job to the fullest. You will have a better value for your time and money. For an added bonus, work in a store where you frequently shop. You can take advantage of the employee discounts.

45
Forget about keeping up with the Joneses. Keep up with your personal budget instead.

46
Avoid heavy stock trading. The fees for commissions and taxes cut into the gains.

47
Never invest in something you know nothing about.

48
Never purchase property you have not seen.

53
Do not hold on to stocks for sentimental reasons. If it is a bad company, 'cut that dog loose'.

54
Do not buy anything simply because it is new and improved. If your current version works, why incur cost for minimal changes?

52
Avoid lending money to friends or relatives. Nine times out of ten, you will either lose the money and/or damage the relationship. If you must lend money to family, secure collateral to ensure a return.

55
Do not spend your pension, 401k or other retirement plan funds when you leave a job. You will lose nearly half of it paying taxes and penalties. Contact an investment professional who can assist you in rolling your plan over to a professionally managed IRA so your money can continue to grow.

56
Pay off all of your debt as quickly as possible. Why have a savings account paying minimal interest while simultaneously paying high interest on a credit card?

50
Avoid timeshare programs. There are no real savings in this program. This is a monthly cost for an implied yearly vacation that you may never take. Then you are stuck with the burden of trying to find relatives or friends to use your timeshare so that you can justify the cost.

51
Avoid buying extravagant gifts for loved ones, friends or even yourself that have no intrinsic value. Buy things that have a use or purpose like this book. (hint, hint)

49
Impulse buying could potentially cost you thousands of dollars yearly. When faced with a large purchase, take time to think about it. Sleep on it. If it is a reputable purchase, it will be there in the morning.

64
Install a climate control device. Some of these devices will cause your air conditioner or heater to turn on 15 minutes before you get home rather than running them all day.

63
In cold climates, insulate your house and wrap the hot water heater. Pay this expense up front and it will save you thousands of dollars in heating bills. Do not say you can't afford to insulate your home unless you feel that you have the money to heat the outdoors surrounding your home.

65
Use personal heaters or fans when the entire house is not occupied.

57
Avoid TV shopping. The convenience instigates impulse buying.

62
If you live by yourself, take in a reliable roommate. Share the costs and utilize your surplus cash to pay off debt.

61
Get several bids for major projects like roofing, re-paving a driveway, installing a patio, etc.

58
Do not buy space in a storage facility. If you are attempting to house useless items or things you no longer use, donate them to a charity.

59
Save your receipts on major purchases. If the item is broken, lost or stolen, the credit card company or merchandise warranty may apply. Also, if applicable, an insurance company will require confirmation of the cost to pay on a claim.

60
Recycle your used items or have a rummage sale.

66
Install basic cable. Why pay for premium channels featuring movies that run all day when you can rent the movies you want to see?

67
Always shop with coupons. Some grocery stores give double value for coupons. However, avoid the habit of buying things just because you have a coupon. Many experimental items end up in the trash.

68
Watch for sales on the grocery items you purchase on a regular basis. For example, I consume a large amount of orange juice and frozen lemonade. When those items are on sale, I buy as many as my freezer will hold. They usually last me until the next time those items are on sale.

69
Check the unit price. Carry a small calculator when shopping, and compare the prices.

74
If you purchase an item and it does not suit its purpose or you really do not like it once you get it home, do not put it in the back of your closet never to be seen again. Take the time to return it and get your money back.

70
Do not allow your children to determine your grocery list. Many times children ask for items that catch their eye on TV but they later end up not consuming the food item. Advertisers appeal to the sense of sight and not always the quality or sense of taste.

73
Make your garments and shoes last. Take care of your clothes by keeping them clean and properly tailored. Put rubber soles and taps on the bottom of your shoes. This will add to their longevity.

72
Be loyal to your service providers. Get to know them. For example, a good dry cleaner will sometimes negotiate a rate if you use them often enough. They will also replace buttons and fix tears for free.

71
Buy clothes off-season. If you buy swimsuits at the end of the summer, they are usually half price. You then have a new suit for the next summer. Or buy your winter coat after the snow season has stopped. There is no longer a demand and you can get a huge discount.

76
Examine your monthly bills. Many times there are overcharges on your account. Contact your provider and challenge the bill. It might result in a credit.

77
Avoid using more than two financial institutions. I knew a man who had four IRA accounts at 4 banks and two different brokerage firms. He was paying a custodial fee at each financial institution. He could have placed them all in one location and saved hundreds of dollars yearly. The consolidation would also cause the generation and review of only one financial statement.

75
Use a gallon jug or large receptacle and start saving your loose change. You would be surprised how much you can accumulate.

79
When you go to purchase a car, bring a calculator. Even if you do not know how to use it, just the sight of you calculating and figuring adds to your negotiating power.

78
There is no law that requires you to carry a monthly car payment. Plan your future car purchase. How do you buy a new car? CASH.

80
Forget the fact that alcohol is expensive, it is not conducive to you becoming a Millionaire. Nobody I know has told me they are successful because they drink.

83
Encourage your college students to buy used textbooks.

81
Avoid dating people with no money. If they are broke while you are dating them, they are displaying their budgeting habits. Remember that there is a difference between someone who is young and struggling to get ahead and someone who is consistently broke.

82
Set up a budget for your children while they are young. You are not their ATM machine.

90
If you are already making an IRA contribution, consider a tax-deferred annuity. There are new annuities without surrender charges. This type of annuity alleviates you from incurring costs for taxes or capital gains and dividends until you reach age 59 ½.

89
Keep your money invested. Too much money is kept in a bank savings account yielding low interest.

91
Make a charitable stock donation to your church or synagogue. If you give stock to your church or synagogue, you get credit for its current market value rather than what you paid for it. You don't have to pay capital gains.

88
Talk to a financial advisor before settling on an insurance policy. Then try to pay yearly or every six months. You can usually get a discount if you pay the full premium rather than monthly installments.

87
Limit the amount of credit cards in your name. I believe two is enough, one personal and one business. However, all of them should be paid off at the end of the month.

92
If you tithe or give money to a church, secure the proper statement from the church to verify the amount. The government will give you tax credit.

84
Encourage your college students to participate in work-study programs. Working part-time while going to school never hurt anyone.

86
Give yourself an allowance. Do not spend haphazardly, using the ATM like a piggy bank. Discipline yourself and live off of your allowance.

85
If your adult children live at home, they should be paying rent. Parents convince themselves that they are 'helping' but in reality, they are handicapping their children. They are creating a false sense of reality. If an adult child pays rent that is comparable to what would be charged by a stranger, the parent can save half and give it as a gift when they are ready to move out. If you do not, they will never move out.

96
If you plan to start a business, write out a business plan. Do research on the venture. Do not enter any venture blindly.

95
Buy beverages and snacks in bulk. Stop worshiping vending machines. Those few dollars accumulate quickly.

94
Pay half of your mortgage payment biweekly rather than the entire payment monthly. Biweekly payments equal 26 payments a year over the standard 12. This plan amounts to 13 full mortgage payments each year. This could reduce thousands off your mortgage and it will certainly have your home paid off at a faster rate. You do not have to carry a mortgage for the rest of your life. You could own it!

97
Do not always treat someone to dinner. Birthdays, business deals, anniversaries, celebrate those occasions over lunch. Lunch entrées are usually $5–$10 less than dinner meals.

93
Keep records of all business and entertainment expenditures. Many people do not take tax credit for mileage, business meals, software purchases etc. I suggest consulting a professional tax advisor on this one.

98
If you must treat someone to dinner, go to a restaurant featuring dinner specials. Take your dinner guest to a "Happy Hour" or "Free Taco Bar". This may raise a few eyebrows but I would take co-workers out for their birthday to a dinner special and pretend to be pleasantly surprised at our "luck".

99
Carry a tip card. Rather than being embarrassed, many people leave a larger tip than necessary.

100
Give stock as a gift on Christmas and Birthdays. Especially to children. This gift will grow with them.

Chapter

III

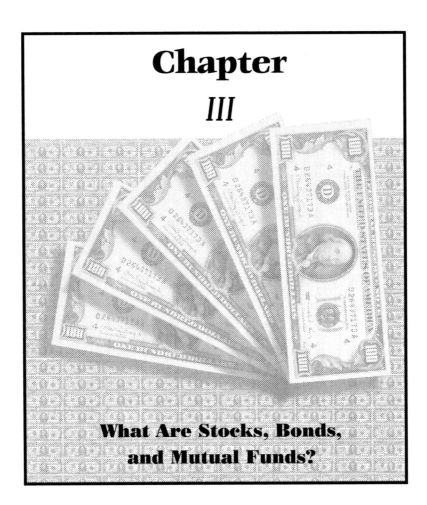

What Are Stocks, Bonds, and Mutual Funds?

TI₂₁ CK₆₄ ER₄₄ TIPS₈₇

The term *blue chip* is a poker term; the blue chip in a poker game is the chip of highest value. Thus, *blue chip stocks* are stocks from well-established, large corporations with extensive records of increased growth and dividends. *Blue chip stocks* historically have produced continuing, moderate growth.

A privately owned company changes to a publicly owned company in order to raise capital. A company raises capital by either issuing **stocks** or **bonds**. When a corporation raises money by issuing stock, it is essentially selling shares or portions of the company to the buyer. Issuing stock is also known as an equity offering.

When you buy a **share** in a company, you own a part of that company. So what does that mean? What is in it for you? Well, if the company is well managed and earns a substantial profit, the value of the stock increases. It is very important to understand that company earnings drive stock prices up. When the stock has a greater value, people are anxious to get a piece of the action. The greater the demand for a stock, the higher the stock price to the new buyer.

When the price of a stock increases and is worth more than what you initially paid, that elevated difference is your profit, or appreciation. You gain tangible appreciation when you sell stock for more than its original price. There is an industry slogan, *buy low and sell high*. I recommend starting a new trend, ***buy all the time and build your empire.***

There is another way to make money on appreciated stock. It is known as obtaining *dividends* from your stock. A dividend is the amount of money a company will pay you for each share of stock you own in their company. The dividends are paid from the company earnings. Usually, the dividends are paid quarterly: every 3 months. These regularly scheduled dividend payments usually come from **blue-chip stocks** that are sometimes referred to as income or dividend paying stock.

As an illustration, based on its profits, a company may decide that it will pay a dividend of $1.25 per share. Let us suppose you have 400 shares and therefore your quarterly dividend check from this company would be $500.00. It is usually recommended that you reinvest dividend payments. However, dividend reinvestment is not always advisable. Some people, such as retirees, plan to use their dividends to supplement their income during their retirement rather than reinvest.

Some companies do not pay dividends, but instead put the money back into the business. These companies are labeled 'growth companies'. Growth companies use the money to invest in research, company expansion or development of new products. Growth companies are preferred when accelerated increase is desired. Growth stocks have a more explosive income potential, but these stocks carry a greater risk.

STOCKS

GOING PUBLIC

You have already learned that when you buy stock, you are buying a share or part of a company. Let us look at an example of a company that goes *public,* which is to sell stock or shares of the company. By the way, this is a true story. A young businessman in his early 30s had always worked with computers. His knowledge of computer technology became well known in his small association of friends and neighbors. As a result, to earn extra money, he began his own computer consulting company. Soon the company's growth reached a point where it was no longer a part-time venture. After a period of time, the company's reputation became well known in his area and it was necessary for the businessman to hire additional staff members to accommodate the growing demand for his services. During these growth periods the businessman would finance the company by taking out small business loans. And although he continued to show a substantial profit at the end of each year, he had dreams of expanding throughout the state and eventually become a nationwide service. In order to do this he needed to take on additional investors. This process is called *going public.*

When a company decides to go from privately owned to publicly owned, executives meet with *investment bankers* who *underwrite,* or buy, all of the company's stock. The *underwriters* make their profit from the difference between purchase price of the company's stock and the amount they sell the stock to the public. The *IPO* or *initial public offering* is the company's first offering to the public. After the *initial public offering,* the stock trades on the open market

TI CK ER TIPS

When you buy a share of a company, you also buy an opportunity to have *voting rights* on how the company is run. The power of your vote depends upon the amount of shares you own. It is not just one person, one vote. It is one person possessing ten shares, producing ten votes.

like all other securities and the price varies depending on expectation of the company's future growth.

The variation in the cost of the stock depends upon the underwriters' projection as to how people will perceive the growth of the company. Whether the public will sense the potential appreciation or the possibility of elevated dividends, or both. Once the initial price of the stock is determined, it is offered to the public for sale, thus, *initial public offering*. After that point, if a lot of people buy the stock, the price goes up. If a lot of people sell their stock, the price goes down. Stock prices are market driven...supply and demand.

One of the key indicators an investor looks for in a company is the company's *price to earnings ratio*, which is the price of the stock, divided by its earnings per share. The higher the *price to earnings ratio,* the more investors are willing to pay. As a result, the investors will expect more earnings growth. A low **price to earnings ratio** may be an indication that a company is in its mature phase and companies with a low *price to earnings ratio* usually have a higher *yield* than companies with high *price to earnings ratios.*

A stock's *yield* is the dividends or income you receive divided by what you invested. A stock's *return* is the difference between the amount of money the stock has increased versus the amount of money you invested; this is usually calculated on an annual basis. Why are stock *yields* and **returns** important? The answer is simple. They measure how your stock is doing. Yield and return answer the question, "Is this *Millionaire-In-Training* exercise really paying off?"

When a company *goes public,* the company selects a Board of Directors who oversee the company and determine how that company is run. The Board of Directors hold an annual meeting to present an annual report and offer initiatives for shareholders' votes. These initiatives could include such items as electing new board members or issuing more stock. Often, shareholders cannot attend a board meeting, so they are sent a *proxy* or absentee ballot. Even if you only own one share of a company, you still have the opportunity to vote on how that company is run.

CERTIFICATE

Proof that you own a stock is issued in the form of a *stock certificate*. The *stock certificate* includes the number of shares, whether the stock is common or preferred, the company's name, and most importantly, your name. In the new age of technology, many companies have eliminated the paper stock certificate; instead, the records are stored electronically in what is known as "street name". This means the stock is not in your name but the name of the brokerage firm that holds your stocks. One advantage to this procedure is that the firm can automatically reinvest your dividends and/or the stock can immediately be sold. Otherwise, using the paper certificate method, you must account for all of your *own* dividends, and you would have to bring the stock certificate back and forth anytime you desire to sell.

Symbols

Week H Lo	Stock Sym	Div	Yld%	PE	Vol 100s	Hi	Lo	Close	Net Change
88 53	Winner.WIN	.64	.9	50	23072	70	68	69	+1

Every stock has an alpha character symbol that represents the company's name. Hypothetically, let us make up a technological company and call it "Winner". The stock symbol will be WIN. This symbol is used in the stock market and on the trading floor to represent our company. So, if you saw the symbol WIN, you would recognize it as our company. The stock symbol is also used in identifying company stock quotes in the newspaper. Let us look at how to read a stock quote in the newspaper.

Every stock on the New York Stock Exchange has 3 symbols or less. We are going to examine our company, Winner. The 52-week high and low is the most and least someone paid for that stock. Dividend is abbreviated "Div.", and represents what a company pays out annually in cash or stock.

Yield—

is the percentage of dividend return on the stock. The 64-cent dividend is .9% of Winner's stock price. As you can see, the lower the stock price and the higher the dividend, the higher the yield.

"PE"—

which is 50, is the price to earnings ratio that we discussed earlier.

Vol. 100s—

is the number of shares traded that day. The number is calculated when you take the number listed, 23,072, and multiply it by 100 to get the total number of shares traded. "Hi" is the highest price that someone paid for the stock that day and "lo" is the lowest price that someone paid for the stock that day.

Close—

is the price at which the stock ended that day.

Net Change—

is the change in the stock price from the day before. Winner closed $1.00 higher than the day before.

BONDS

ISSUING

As mentioned previously, the second way for a company to raise money is a bond offering. Many people don't realize that the bond market is significantly larger than the stock market in terms of dollar volume traded. When you buy a bond, you are loaning a corporation your money. In exchange, the corporation pays you an agreed upon percentage of *interest* on your loan, and returns your loan at an agreed upon time or *maturity date*.

When an individual buys a stock, they are buying a share of the company and can earn money through dividends and appreciation. When an individual buys a bond, they are not buying a share of a company. They earn money by receiving an annual interest on their *principal*, which is the amount of money they originally paid for the bond.

Corporations or municipalities, state and federal government agencies, issue bonds. After a company or government decides to finance a project by **issuing** a bond, they negotiate with potential investment bankers to select an investment banker who will **underwrite**, which means to purchase all of the bonds and then resell the bonds to investors.

OBLIGATIONS

Bonds are often called *obligations* because the corporation or agency is obligated to repay the *par value*, that is to say, the amount paid for the bond, and an agreed upon interest rate. The company is obligated to pay bond holders first, preferred stock holders next, and common stock holders last.

A company may prefer to sell bonds rather than stocks because the issuing of more stock could dilute the value of already existing stock. Bonds can also be sold on the *secondary market.* This means that after a bond has been sold with a specific interest rate and a specific maturity date, the investor might decide to sell his or her bond to someone else, this becomes a **secondary market** buy.

INTEREST PAYMENTS

There are several factors that are taken into account when determining the rate of interest on bonds. One of the major factors is bond rating. The two primary companies that rate bonds are *Standard & Poor's* and *Moody's.* These companies provide information about the soundness of a company, not the soundness of the bond market. The ratings are based on how risky the corporation or agency is perceived to be. The risk is whether or not the company can pay the annual *interest* and the *par value* at *maturity.*

The higher the interest rate. The higher the risk of the bond. People invest in the bond market because it tends to have a lower risk compared to stocks. However, *junk or high yield bonds* pay higher interest than the government can, but as a result, they are riskier. One major downside of buying bonds is that inflation may outpace your interest rate and significantly reduce your purchasing power.

MATURITY DATE

The *maturity date* of a bond is the date payment on the bond is due. The date that the company or agency has agreed to repay your principal. Maturity dates range from 1 month to 30 years. The longer the *maturity date* the higher the *interest rate*. If an investor's money is tied up over a long period of time, *inflation* could reduce the value of their *principle.* In other words you are paid at a higher rate to wait to get your return on investment.

CLASSIFICATION

There are three major types of bonds: corporate, government and government agency. Corporate bonds are classified as **short term**, 1-5 years; **intermediate-term**, 5-10 years, and **long-term**, 10-20 years. Some bonds are **callable**. This means that a company can buy its bonds back before the maturity date. When the bond is issued, the first time the bond could be **recalled** or **redeemed** is listed. A company may want to redeem its bonds if interest rates go significantly lower than what they are paying their investors. The company can call the bond and reissue bonds at a lower rate, thus saving significant dollars for the company. Calling a bond is similar to refinancing your house; you bring in your loan and get a cheaper loan.

MUTUAL FUNDS

SOURCE OF MUTUAL FUNDS

When you buy mutual funds, you are pooling your money with other investors to buy securities. You and other people with a common goal, hire an investment manager and he/she does all the driving. For a small fee, the investment manager invests your money for you and for others like you.

A mutual fund can be compared to riding a bus. Its destination or objective is written on the front of the bus. First, you select a driver (fund manager). Upon boarding, you pay a fee. Fasten your seatbelt and get ready for the ride. The driver/fund manager directs the bus/fund for you. You go up when the bus/fund goes up; you go down when the bus/fund goes down. The secret to a prosperous ride is staying on the bus and not jumping out at every speed bump or stall. *As Millionaires-in-Training,* we stay on the bus and add gas monthly (dollar cost averaging), so we can go farther. The more gas we put in, the farther we go. How do *Millionaires-in-Training ride* the bus? Confidently! *Millionaires-in-Training* stay on for the long ride.

How can a financial advisor help you with your ride? A financial advisor can help you to decide which bus to take and to measure the risk of the ride. A financial advisor is also there to keep you on course when you consider getting off. He or she is like a tour guide; they can answer questions, monitor performance, reassure in stormy times, or adjust strategy when you arrive at a detour. Detours include such route changes as marriage, divorce, unemployment, children, college planning, or retirement planning.

What's the cost of the bus ride? When you pay your bus fare in advance, the fee is called a *front-end load.* When you pay your fare upon departure, the fee is called a *back-end load.* In a *back-end load,* the longer you ride the bus, the lower the fare when you get off. When you get on the bus with no advisor, no entry fee, or no exit fee, it is called a *no-load.* However, a *no-load* does have a charge. You are charged a $12.00 fee that is used to pay for sales, marketing, management and trading costs.

Another option that is becoming more popular is called *level-load*. In a *level-load*, you pay nothing to get in and nothing to get out as long as you hold the fund for 12 months; otherwise, you pay a 1% redemption fee. The level-load is popular because you get in with no up-front costs and you still get financial advice.

THE BENEFITS

There are many benefits associated with Mutual Funds. Too few people take advantage of this strategy because of their lack of knowledge. As we mentioned, you and investors like you are pooling your money to purchase securities. This tactic affords you the opportunity of sharing ownership in several different companies. Let us explore Mutual Fund benefits further.

1

Professional Management

You have a professional manager that is well versed in investing. Few people have the knowledge or time to study and analyze stocks, economic conditions and trends. It is wiser to hire a person or a team to manage your money. A mutual fund manager makes 'buy and sell' decisions and they have the benefit of many analysts and strategists. In other words, *you don't have to be an expert to invest; you just have to know one.*

2

Diversification

An advantage you have with a mutual fund is that when you invest, you are diversified over many companies. A mutual fund may own as many as 100 companies. You can own dozens of securities, which would normally be too expensive to purchase individually. You could invest in many sectors with one mutual fund. For example, if you own one security, when it goes down, you go down. On the other hand, if you owned several companies, when one of those companies goes down, it would have a minor impact on your entire portfolio.

3

Convenience

If you own a mutual fund, you are given a statement and periodic paperwork pertaining to the status of the fund from the firm holding your mutual fund. When tax time rolls around, you are sent a statement containing all capital gains and dividend information. You can reinvest profits back into the fund for free (there will be an illustration of this later). You can invest into the fund monthly. Also, most mutual funds have a family of funds. As your objectives change you can switch to a different fund within the family and not incur a sales charge. Mutual funds can also be put in brokerage accounts, IRA, Roth IRA's,401ks, 403b7,s and other retirement plans.

4
Regulation

The Investment Company Act of 1940 contains a myriad of rules that mutual funds (investment companies) have to abide by. There are also several other federal and state laws that mutual funds must adhere to. The Securities and Exchange Commission (SEC) oversee them. This regulation is designed to protect investors by requiring mutual funds to clearly define the risks of investing, to report performance consistently, to operate within prescribed standards and to observe anti-fraud rules in the buying and selling of fund shares.

5
Liquidity

Open-end mutual funds can be redeemed at Net Asset Value (NAV). Net Asset Value is like the net worth of a mutual fund. It is calculated at the end of the trading day by taking all the securities in the mutual fund portfolio and dividing them by the shares outstanding. That number is the NAV. The mutual fund company will calculate that for you. Best of all, you can sell it at any time. After the NAV is calculated, that amount is sent to you less any sales charges, if any. Your mutual fund company will sell it upon request. It takes 3 days to settle the account and then a check is mailed to you. Your check should be received within 7 business days after a sale.

6
Discipline

One of the aspects I encourage most is discipline. Eliminate the process of buy and sell decisions. You just invest monthly and let the fund manager buy and sell for you. When the market is down most first time investors do not have the intestinal fortitude to buy or to hold onto securities. You have a manager doing that for you. You simply do your part and invest monthly then hold on for the long haul.

7
Affordable

Mutual funds have low initial costs. You can start with as little as $250 or a low monthly investment of $50 a month. With those funds, you get a diversified, regulated, convenient, liquid and professionally managed portfolio. This is probably one of the best ways for investors to leverage their time and knowledge.

There are several different types of mutual funds. At last count, there were over 9,000 mutual funds. There are more mutual funds than stocks on the New York Stock Exchange. The best fund for you is determined by your risk tolerance and by your time horizon. Like anything else, the higher the risk, the higher the return.

If you have to pay for your child's education within the next three months, then putting your money in the stock market would not be a good idea. That would be like taking a plane to travel three blocks. If you were saving for your retirement and it is 10 years away, keeping your money in a money market would not be a wise utilization of your money. That would be like walking from Los Angeles to New York and back again. We must choose the right investment to make our lives easier, efficient and more profitable.

TYPES OF MUTUAL FUND INVESTMENTS

The following list includes types of investments, from the most conservative to the most aggressive type of investing:

1

Money market. . .

funds are for the short-term investor. Money market funds invest in CDs, treasury bills and commercial paper. The maturity rate for a money market fund is 12 months or less. However, the government or FDIC does not guarantee money market funds. The share of each fund is always $1.00 per share; the interest rate on a money market fund is the only thing that fluctuates. This type of investment is one step above a passbook savings. This is equivalent to *strolling*.

2

Municipal bond funds. . .

have a tax free status if purchased in the state in which you reside. Municipalities issue municipal bonds. Municipal bonds tend to pay the lowest interest of all the bonds; however, with the money you save in taxes, the municipal bond raises your return. In the investment world it is called tax equivalent yield (TEY). For example, if you bought a bond yielding 3.5% and you were in the 38% tax bracket, you would have to do 5.5% in a similar bond, with similar risk, just to break even with the 3.5% municipal. This 5.5% includes California State tax. This is equivalent to *walking*.

3

Government bond funds. . .

generally invest in government securities. Government bond funds may include US Treasury issues and mortgage-backed securities like Fannie Maes and Ginnie Maes. In corporate bonds, the fund purchases corporate bonds issued by companies. These rates vary the most in interest because they not only fluctuate by current interest rates but by the credit of the company. When you buy corporate bond funds, check the credit quality in the prospectus or ask your financial consultant which corporate bond fund would be best for you. If you choose to hold high yield bonds or corporate bonds, make sure you understand the risk you incur compared to your interest. Bonds are similar to ***riding a bike***; it's faster than walking, but not as fast as driving.

4

Balanced mutual funds. . .

have the lowest risk and lowest return of equity funds. Balanced funds have a mix of stocks, bonds and cash equivalent investments. It pays a higher yield than all stock funds, which is good in a falling market. But when the market goes up, the balanced fund does not go as high because it contains bonds. It is less risky than an all stock mutual funds, but more risky than an all bond fund. It is sometimes referred to as the 50/50 method. You outpace inflation and get the growth that stocks provide; also you get the stability of a high quality company and government issues. This is a conservative route, like driving a car ***35 mph.***

5

Growth and income funds. . .

are one of my favorite areas. It does exactly what it says, growth with steady income. What growth and income mutual funds do is to invest in large US companies that have been in business for decades and have long records of increased earnings and dividends. These are the companies you use every day and here is your chance to profit from them. Growth and income funds are inflation killers because your expenses are not fixed. The market can go up, down or sideways; in all three market trends, growth and income funds provide dividends. This is like ***driving 50-60 mph.***

6

Growth funds. . .

usually invest in large to medium companies whose long-term earnings are expected to grow more rapidly than other companies. In other words, they are trying to pick the best and the brightest with little regard to dividends. The dividends are considered secondary in stock appreciation. This is like driving a little faster than in the growth and income fund. These are your high-flying stock. If you want a return this is how you proceed, but make sure you can handle bumps and bruises. Aggressive growth companies invest in small companies that are believed to grow very rapidly; you are getting in on the ground floor or expansion phase of a company. This is like *driving 60-70 mph.*

7

Global funds. . .

invest all over the world including the United States. International funds only invest overseas at non-US based companies. Global and international funds have to deal with currency-exchange risk. These are the highest of all risk investments. *This is like driving 65-75 mph.*

Chapter
IV

How The Market Works?

HISTORICAL OVERVIEW

Many people think that if they have knowledge of the origin of an entity, the entity will be easier to understand. So, let us observe a historical overview of the origin of the stock market. Once upon a time, in 1792, twenty-four men stood around under a buttonwood tree on New York's Wall Street where they traded stocks. The street was called Wall Street because the early settlers had built a stockade to protect   New York from Indian and pirate attacks from the

The NYSE is considered to be the most prestigious exchange and includes the larger, older and more financially sound companies; there are approximately 1,600 companies listed.

The American Stock Exchange was established in 1842 and was originally called the New York Curb Exchange; the name was changed in 1953. Smaller and younger companies are listed on the AMEX, which lists about 890 companies.

The OTC market trades stocks that are from young, upstart companies, and usually have the fastest growth rate. Financial institutions are also listed on the OTC marketplace. Many of the high tech companies are listed on the OTC market. This is the largest trading market with approximately 31,000 companies listed.

north. These 24 men soon moved their business indoors, and thus the New York Stock Exchange was born.

Today, the three most common ways that individual investors trade stocks in the United States are: (1) New York Stock Exchange (NYSE); (2) American Stock Exchange (AMEX); and (3) Over the Counter Stock (OTC) market. It is considered prestigious for a company to be traded on a stock exchange because the company has to meet specific criteria in order to be listed on the exchange. The criteria for being listed on a specific exchange includes the company's earnings, assets, number of shares outstanding, number of stockholders, and number of stockholders who hold at least 100 shares.

STOCK MARKET

HOW A STOCK GETS TO MARKET
Before we look specifically at how the stock market works, let's do a quick, three-step review of what you have learned so far.

REVIEW
A privately owned company decides that it needs to raise capital. One way to do so is to sell stock. That stock is traded on the exchange. An investor selects a broker and together they agree on an appropriate investment strategy. Jointly, the broker and the investor analyze his or her financial goals and decide whether growth or income stocks best suits his or her needs. The investor is now ready to go to market. Anytime during market hours, a person can buy or sell stocks.

The New York Stock Exchange (NYSE) is located in New York City; the American Stock Exchange (AMEX) is located in New York City as well; and the Over the Counter marketplace is found on computers all over the world.

> **TI₂₁CK₆₄ER₄₄ TIPS₈₇**
>
> Stock is usually sold in *round lots,* that is groups of 100 shares. Stocks not bought in **round lots** are considered *odd lots,* or groups of stocks not in multiples of 100.

Remember that a stock exchange does not set the prices of stocks. The investors set the prices. The market is driven by supply and demand. If you really look at it, the various markets are the sum intelligence of everyone in the world. Some people make good decisions, some people make bad decisions. Each time a stock is traded, there is a winner and a loser. If you buy ABC company from someone for $50 a share and it goes up to $100 per share, you are the winner in that transaction.

NOW WE ARE READY TO TRADE. . .

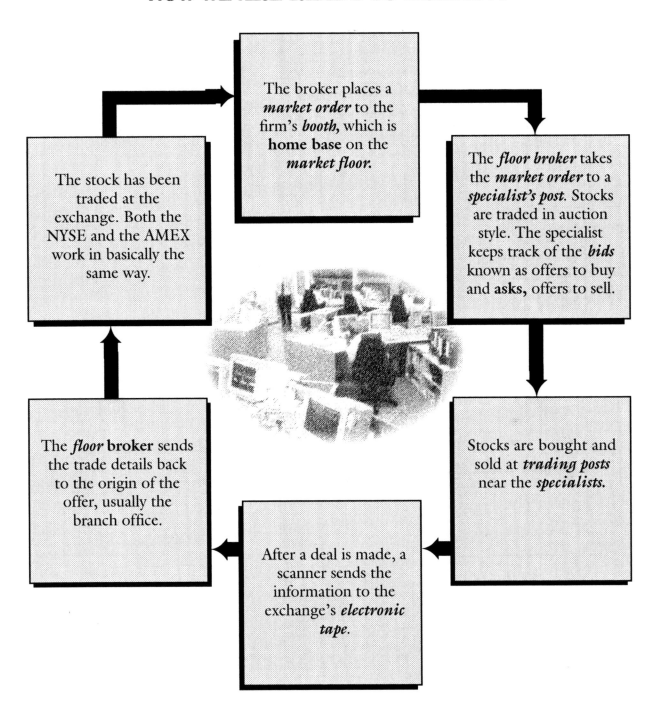

The broker places a *market order* to the firm's **booth**, which is **home base** on the *market floor.*

The *floor broker* takes the *market order* to a *specialist's post.* Stocks are traded in auction style. The specialist keeps track of the *bids* known as offers to buy and **asks,** offers to sell.

The stock has been traded at the exchange. Both the NYSE and the AMEX work in basically the same way.

Stocks are bought and sold at *trading posts* near the *specialists.*

The *floor* **broker** sends the trade details back to the origin of the offer, usually the branch office.

After a deal is made, a scanner sends the information to the exchange's *electronic tape.*

The stock transactions of the NYSE are listed in the Wall Street Journal and are also listed in most major local newspapers.

To obtain a membership or *seat* on the New York Stock Exchange, the *seat* is purchased. Having a seat on the exchange translates into having the ability to trade stock at the exchange. Like stocks, the cost of a seat is driven by supply and demand. There are only a limited amount of seats on the exchange. In order for an individual or institution to purchase a seat, someone has to sell his or her position. For example in January 1987, a seat on the NYSE cost $1.1 million. As of June 1999, a seat costs $2.3 million dollars. The seat has increased in value because no one wants to relinquish his or her right to trade at the exchange. There is a greater demand for that position.

SECURITIES AND EXCHANGE COMMISSION

The Securities and Exchange Commission was established by the US Government in 1934 to protect the public from any wrong doings in the trading of securities. The commission consists of 5 persons who are appointed by the President of the United States for 5-year terms on a rotating basis. No more than three of the appointees can be from the same political party.

The Over the Counter stocks are not traded at an exchange. The stocks are traded over the phone and recorded electronically. The computer network for these electronic transfers is called the National Market System, (*NMS*). The organization that regulates the OTC market

is the *National Association of* **Securities** *Dealers, NASD.* The transactions of the most actively traded stock are listed in the *National Association of Securities Dealers Automated Quotations, NASDAQ.*

Trading on the stock exchanges or in the over the counter market place all have one thing in common, they are market driven; again, it is all about supply and demand. This is where sentiment kicks in. If the majority of investors feel good about the market, then it goes up; and if they feel bad about the market, it goes down. This causes the day-to-day fluctuations.

HOW THE BOND MARKET WORKS

Bonds trade at par, discount, or premium. Let's say Sue buys a bond at par $1,000 at 5% rates and bonds have a converse relationship. When interest rates go up, bond prices go down. It is like a teeter-totter, one goes up causing the other to go down. When Sue buys a 5% bond and interest rates change, the bond is not immediately re-priced; the bond adjusts in the bond market.

For example, if her bonds are at 5% and interest rates go up to 7%, she can not sell her bond at 5% a par ($1,000) because why would someone buy her bond at 5% when the market is paying 7%, which could mean $200 more a year. She would have to sell her bonds for less to make up the difference; this is called selling at discount.

On the other hand, if interest rates went down to 3.5 % what would happen to Sue's bonds? The bonds would go up. Why? If everyone is paying 3.5% for their bonds and Sue is holding a 5% bond, people are going to pay more to get Sue's bond. Thus, Sue would receive a premium for her bonds.

A QUICK REVIEW OF HOW A BOND GETS TO THE MARKET:

Issuer
A company, federal or local government, or government agency decides to raise **capital** by **issuing a bond.**

Underwriter
An investment banker, or **underwriter**, buys all of the bonds and then reissues the bonds to the public.

Investor
You, the investor buy a bond and in return you earn **interest** on the bond and receive the full amount you paid known as the **principal,** at a specified time known as the **maturity** date.

Interest divided by the price paid for the bond is the **bond yield**. Bond yields are lower than stock yields, although, this has not always been the case. In 1945 the yield on stocks was almost twice the yield on bonds. The yield differential reversed in the early 1960s when the yield on stocks became twice the yield on bonds.

THE THREE TYPES OF BONDS

1) CORPORATIONS ISSUE [CORPORATE BONDS].
Corporations often prefer to issue a bond rather than issue stock to raise capital, because the issuing of new stock could reduce the value of stock that has already been issued.

2) FEDERAL, STATE AND LOCAL GOVERNMENTS CAN ISSUE GOVERNMENT BONDS.
One reason people invest in bonds rather than invest in stock is because they get a tax advantage from bond investments because all money earned from stocks is taxable on the federal and state level.

US TREASURY BONDS. . .
are taxable at the federal level but are tax-free at the state or local level. State or local government bonds known as **municipal bonds** or **"munis"** are tax-free if you buy them in the state where you live. For example, if you lived in California and bought bonds in New York, you would have to pay state tax. It is particularly advantageous for people in the upper income tax brackets to invest in **municipal bonds** because their **yield** is increased since they don't pay taxes on the interest they make.

3) GOVERNMENT AGENCY BONDS. . .
are issued by federal and state government agencies. For example, the Government National Mortgage Association (GNMA also called Ginnie Maes) provides money for mortgages.

Bonds can be purchased at the stock exchanges or banks. The New York Stock Exchange and the American Stock Exchange both have bond rooms where bonds are traded auction style. You can also buy bonds at your bank, and US Treasury bonds can be purchased through a broker or directly from the Federal Reserve Bank. Most bonds, like stocks, are bought in the over the counter market.

Bond listings are located in the same newspaper section as stock listings. The upside to buying bonds is that there is less risk than in stocks because you know what specific income or interest you will get; you can also do better planning because you know when the principal will mature, and of course, there are the tax advantages.

The downside to buying bonds is that the rate of inflation may outpace your interest rate and the bond may be called. At that point, the corporate bond issuer could *default* the bond interest or principal; and it usually takes a great deal of capital to buy bonds with minimums ranging from $1,000 to $10,000.

HOW THE MUTUAL FUND MARKET WORKS

Today, there are more mutual funds than there are stocks listed on the New York Stock Exchange. This was not always the case. The mutual fund market began 75 years ago. In 1924, a group of Boston investors founded the Massachusetts Investors Trust. The fund was a private investment firm for the founders. The fund is still around, however, with several major changes. The fund is now open to everyone and they have a whole family of funds. I will show you an illustration of the fund later when I explain the power of compound interest, investing monthly, and the discipline of investing over the long haul.

The dollar volume of investments in mutual funds has also experienced significant growth. For example, in 1941, there was one half billion dollars invested in mutual funds; in 1961 there was 3.5 billion dollars invested in mutual funds; and in 1999 there were over 5 trillion dollars according to the Investment Company Institute. I believe the massive growth in mutual funds is due to the baby boomers putting money away for retirement. Imagine all the people and companies putting money into their retirement plans 401k, 403bs and pensions. It is mind-boggling.

POOLED MONEY
A mutual fund company decides upon its investment objectives; issues a prospectus, and sells shares. A group of Millionaires-in-Training, and other investors combine their money to buy shares from the mutual fund. There are three ways to invest in mutual funds: through a mutual fund company, brokerage, or bank.

EXPERT MANAGEMENT
The investor along with the financial consultant analyzes his or her financial goals and decide on the type of fund to invest in: growth funds e.g., stock; income funds, e.g., bonds; or growth and income funds, e.g., stocks and bonds.

DIVERSIFICATION
Diversification is an important strategy to successful investing. If your portfolio includes a wide variety of securities, you are less vulnerable to losses. Your losses could be offset by your gains. A mutual fund provides the resources for investing in a wide variety of securities.

HOW MUTUAL FUNDS GET TO MARKET

In review, mutual funds are so popular because it is so easy to get into the market. Other factors that contribute to the success of the mutual fund market are the mutual funds' diversification and expert management. Here is a three-step process on how mutual funds get to market:

BUYING MUTUAL FUNDS

While some mutual funds are traded on the stock exchange, most mutual funds are bought directly from a mutual fund company. You buy, a brokerage, or a bank. Banks are legally prohibited from selling mutual funds directly, banks invest your money through affiliations with mutual fund companies.

When you invest in mutual fund companies you are buying shares in a particular fund not buying shares of the mutual fund company itself. You deal directly with the mutual fund company or have your broker deal with the mutual fund company for you. The minimum cost to invest in a mutual fund is $250; however, many funds require a higher startup rate. There are some that will let you start with as little as $50 with the stipulation of investing monthly. Your financial consultant will invest in **closed-end** or **open-end** funds. When mutual funds first started, they were primarily **closed-end** meaning they were only allowed to have the original investors and the original capital. When you have a closed-ended mutual fund it comes out once like an IPO, then it trades on an exchange at a discount or premium based on supply and demand. The mutual funds traded today are open-end, the capital and investors change daily. You can not trade **open-end** funds in the stock market.

The cost of each share of the fund is whatever the **net asset value (NAV)** of the fund is at the time you buy into the fund. An easy way to think of the net asset value is the **net worth** of the fund. All assets are divided by the amount of shares outstanding. Don't worry, you don't have to calculate that quotient everyday. The calculation is done at the close of the market, Monday through Friday at 4:30 Eastern Standard Time. The NAV is also quoted daily in most newspapers.

With all mutual funds you will pay fees. The fee depends upon what type of fund it is and how it is managed. The fee is subtracted from the total assets. Some funds also have a **12B-1 fee** for marketing and distributing the fund. The marketing of mutual funds consists of running ads in the financial press, releasing press announcements, or distributing direct mailings. You can check a fund's fees and performance before you buy into the fund.

Before you buy into a mutual fund, you should go over the prospectus with a financial advisor. The fund's prospectus will inform you of the fund's objectives, fees, risk analysis, and performance. There are approximately 4,000 fund groups. There is a fund to suit anyone's objectives. As noted, you select a fund based upon your investment objective, risk tolerance and time horizon.

Your mutual fund will mail you information about the types of securities in your mutual fund portfolio. Your **portfolio of investments** will identify the type of securities you own, the type of stocks by industries, the name of the stock, the number of shares owned, and the value of your holdings. The mutual fund will also issue a quarterly and annual fund report. These publications list the assets owned by the company at the time of publication.

When a mutual fund company owns a variety of funds, that variety is called a **family of funds**. It is easy to transfer your money between **a family of funds** and there is usually no transfer cost. The investor receives two types of payouts from mutual funds. These payouts are called **distributions.** You receive a monthly **dividend distribution** or a **capital distribution** when you sell your shares in the mutual fund. You can **redeem** or sell your mutual fund shares back to a closed-end or open-end mutual fund company at any time. As a result, the mutual fund company keeps some of the fund's assets in cash.

You evaluate the performance of your mutual fund by the fund's **yield** and **return**. The **NAV yield** and **return** of a mutual fund is calculated at the end of each business day. The fund's performance is listed in newspapers along with other financial listings. Now that we've reviewed what securities are and how the financial markets work, let's explore investment strategies.

Chapter
V

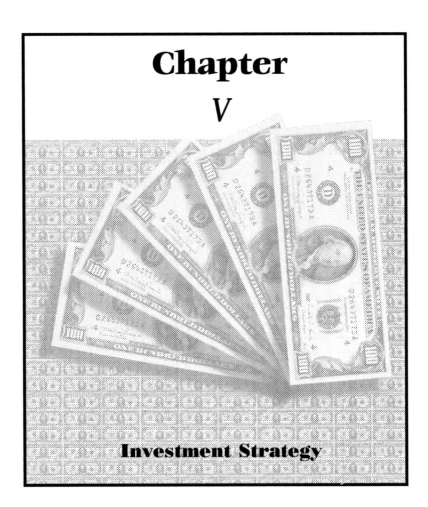

Investment Strategy

**It's a bird,
It's a plane,
It's Millionaire Man**

The investment strategies in this chapter may sound familiar; however, if you do not use your M.I.N.D., they will not be effective. We will examine several strategies for stocks, bonds and mutual funds. Beginning with stocks, the question I am most often asked is, "what stock should I buy or how should I pick a stock?" This basic question is very common among untrained investors. However, choosing the right investment is an extremely determinant factor. A sound stock pick could mean the difference between vacationing at a Villa in the South of France or pitching a tent in the backyard. The first thing you need to do when choosing the right investment is to develop a new vision.

NEW EYES

At this point, you are wondering, why do I need 'new eyes'? What's wrong with the familiar brown eyes that have kept me from walking into walls for so many years? "New eyes" require that you look at things differently. "New eyes" require that you raise your quality of analysis. I call your "new eyes" *millionaire vision*.

If you had one million dollars, what companies would you buy? If that number is too vast, how about one hundred thousand dollars or even more simplistic, what if you were handed ten thousand tax-free dollars? Before you head out to your favorite department store, the stipulation on this gift is that you use it only to invest. What companies would you choose? *Millionaire vision* will cause you to look at *companies*, not *stock companies*. In other words, don't contemplate only the stock prices; consider the status of the company.

There are three major attributes that I look for in a company: *dominance, innovation, and great products/services*. Think of companies that are dominant in their industry. Who are the leaders in producing innovative products or services? Which companies are always ahead of the pack? What corporations are held up as an example of excellence in management and professionalism? This is our starting point.

Now, think of a product or service that many people use. For example, many people have high blood pressure. What company provides the product to alleviate the symptoms caused by high blood pressure? Look at how many people a day shave, brush their teeth, use soap, credit cards, phones, software, and drive cars. Has your millionaire vision heightened? Do you see our purpose? Instead of only *using* all of these products, we can *own* the companies that make them.

For example, I was asked to give a stock pick. At that time, I told this story. A man wakes up in the morning and turns off his *ABC* electric clock; then gets out from under the covers he bought from *DEF* department store; then takes a shower with *GHI* soap; and shaves with *JKL* razor. When he goes downstairs to eat breakfast, he turns on *MN* coffee maker and uses *OP* coffee; with his orange juice he take his daily medication from *QRS* pharmaceutical company; and turns on *TUV* Television set to watch the morning news. Next, he gets into his *W* car, made with *X* metal, drives on *Y* tires, and gets a cellular phone call using *Z* service. We can go through the alphabet naming company products that are used daily before you even leave the house. Before reading further, take a moment to list the names of some of the company products you use each day. After listing these companies, referring back to our initial criterion, are these companies leaders in their industry? Once you have identified those corporations, you have just compiled a list of viable stock picks.

INVESTING IN COMMON STOCK

When you purchase stock you are buying ownership into a company or business. If you own a piece of this company, wouldn't you want the best your money could buy? If you are going to bungy jump, you don't want to invest in the cheapest cord from a fly by night company so that you can save a few dollars. You might want to have a quality cord, manufactured by a long-

> **MILLIONAIRE MOMENT**
>
> There is a distinct difference between "cheap" and undervalued. Cheap is a penny stock (under $5.00). Undervalued is when a good company stock is trading for less than its worth.

standing company and perhaps spend a little more money on the purchase. Some people want to buy certain stock "because it's cheap". The stock is cheap for a reason. People buy cheap stock not realizing that it could go "bluelight".

- What beverages do you drink? •
- What computer do you use at home or at the office? •
- Who makes the chips that run your PC? •
- What software is on the computer? •
- What brand of foods do you eat? •
- Who makes your stationary? •
- What telephone company or cellular phone company do you use? •
- What brand of clothes do you wear? •
- Which company provides the medication you use? •
- Which company supplies the metal for your car? •
- Which company holds the credit cards you use? •

Consequently, we need to purchase ownership into good, solid companies. Especially when you first start investing. Large US companies that you are familiar with should be your focus objective. Let's explore the companies that produce items you own and use:

If you have children, you are looking at another realm entirely. Our product list could range from diapers to special designer water. If you have children, add their products to your list. Has your millionaire vision improved? If so, the next step is intrinsic value.

INTRINSIC VALUE

Intrinsic value is when someone sells something at a premium. For example, when tennis shoes are made for less than $10 a pair and they are sold for over $100 a pair, the difference between $10.00 and $100.00 is the **intrinsic value** of the product. When someone will pay a premium for your product or service, you have a strategic advantage.

To illustrate **intrinsic value** further, let me tell you the story of my relatives who came from out-of-state to visit me in Los Angeles. We decided to go to a national amusement park. When we got there, to gain entry, it cost $30.00 per person. Once inside, with my millionaire vision, I noticed many of the other tourists buying $70.00 sweatshirts and tank tops. My millionaire vision also spied out tourists purchasing $3.00 soft drinks to chase their $6.00 hamburgers. I asked myself, "Could I invite people over to my house and charge $30.00 to come in, serve hot-dogs and soda for $10.00, and put my face on a sweatshirt and sell it for $70.00?" I decided the only way I could buy into this scenario is to buy stock in the company. So, I did. Frequently, you have to fine-tune your millionaire vision while using your M.I.N.D. to get ahead.

OTHER KEY POINTS

As you become more astute in the investment game, you must not only *see* great products; you must look at the management of the company. For instance, do the managers own stock in the company? Does senior management purchase company stock? Does their employee compensation package include employee stock or stock options? The confidence placed in a company by its employees speaks volumes about that company. If the employees do not have a conviction about their product or service, chances are the product is not worth your investment dollars. So, take the time to investigate a company and the faith its personnel places in their organization. This information can be found in the corporation's annual report.

You should also know if the company has a strong earnings **record**. Does the company have a long track record of increased **earnings** and **dividends** with a strong **cash flow** and a high **return on equity**? If the answer is yes, this is a company we should consider as an investment option. Do you know what drives stock prices up?

Not hot tips from your friends. If you are not going to do your homework, you might as well use "eenie, meenie, miney, moe". Earnings is another key reason in determining your stock purchase.

ASSET ALLOCATION

After selecting the leading corporations for your stock purchase, how do we allocate these companies? The way to allocate companies is called *asset allocation*, which is to put money or assets in different sectors to reduce risk. In other words, don't put all of your eggs in one basket. In the real estate market, they say location, location, location. In the stock market, we say diversification, diversification, diversification.

One of the biggest problems faced by investors is not practicing diversification. Once I had a man come to my office, and after reviewing his portfolio, I mentioned diversification. He said, "My stocks are diversified. I have ABC software, DEF technology, GHI computers, and JKL Internet provider." As you can see, his stock portfolio was not diversified at all. Altogether, his companies were in the technology sector. When the tide went up, all of his stocks went up. When the tide went down, his entire future was slammed into the rocks.

Money flows into different financial sectors at different times. A case in point, money can flow out of the financial sector and into the technology sector; out of the technology sector and into the health-care sector. Over a short period of time money could flow out of the health-care sector and into the consumer cyclical sector; out of the consumer cyclical sector and into the energy and utility sector. Without warning, it could flow out of the utility and energy sector and into the telecom sector; and out of the telecom sector into the financial stock sector.

The anti-millionaires are constantly trying to chase the market flow and they often end up buying at higher prices. As Millionaires-in-Training, we diversify our investments and add to our investments monthly. *Time in* the market is more important than *timing* the market. To circumvent this common problem, we buy the best company in every sector. We buy the best in technology, telecom, healthcare, consumer cyclicals and energy. We are building an empire, not putting together a pup tent.

Here are some disciplines I use in diversifying a portfolio:

- Buy quality companies. Companies that dominate their industry;
  have good earnings and great products.
  Avoid investing in penny stocks.

- Don't have more than 15% of your money in one security.

- Don't have more than 30% of your money in any one sector or industry.

THE DOW DIVIDEND STRATEGY

The Dow Dividend Strategy is an easy, time-tested strategy to invest in high quality companies when they are undervalued. First, the Dow Jones Industrial Average is comprised of 30 companies that have been chosen by the editors of the Wall Street Journal. The 30 companies are widely held by individual institutions. I like to think of the 30 companies as the heartbeat of America.

The Dow Jones Industrial Average was founded by Charles Dow and Edward Jones to inform people of daily market performance. The Dow is used as a bench mark for the overall market and includes companies from different sectors, such as: consumer cyclicals, consumer staples, financial, energy, telecom and technology. When you hear someone ask, "how was the market today?" If the response is "up or down 100 points", they are referring to the Dow.

HERE ARE THE 30 COMPANIES THAT MAKE UP THE DOW JONES INDUSTRIAL AVERAGE:

1. Allied Signal
2. Aluminum Co. of America (ALCOA)
3. American Express
4. AT and T
5. Boeing
6. Caterpillar
7. Citigroup
8. Coca-Cola
9. DuPont
10. Eastman Kodak
11. Exxon
12. General Electric
13. General Motors
14. Hewlett Packard
15. Home Depot
16. IBM
17. Intel
18. International Paper
19. Johnson and Johnson
20. J.P. Morgan
21. McDonalds
22. Merck Pharmaceuticals
23. Microsoft
24. 3M
25. Phillip Morris
26. Proctor and Gamble
27. SBC Communications
28. United Technology
29. Wal-Mart
30. Walt Disney

HOT TIPS/COOL INVESTMENTS

Here is a hot tip for a cool investment strategy: buy the ten highest yielding stocks. The lowest stock price with the highest dividend creates the highest yield. Why is this a good strategy?

1. **Performance**
   Over a 25 year period, the strategy to buy the ten highest yielding stocks has out performed the Dow Jones Industrial Average and Standard and Poor's 500 Index (12/31/98)*.

   Dow Dividend 16.78 %
   DJIA   14.40 %
   S & P 500   14.71 %

2. **High Quality**
   Buy high quality, undervalued companies. Try to choose companies that receive a dividend.

3. **High Yielding Stock**
   The ten highest yielding stocks can be bought inside of a unit investment trust. This would eliminate the necessity for buy and sell decisions. The trust could make it more affordable than if you bought the shares individually. Another reward for using the trust is that each year the portfolio has a renewal option. This discipline strategy affords you the luxury of always owning the ten highest dividend-paying companies. The trust will annually separate from the companies that are reducing in yield and replace them with the companies that are paying the highest dividends. Consequently, you will always retain the top dividend paying companies on the Dow.

4. **Stability**
   Investing in the 10 highest yielding stocks has never lost money over any 3-year period. To reap the benefits of a sound investment such as this, you must maintain consistency. Steady retention of this type of investment is necessary as the renewal opportunity occurs annually. This is another example of how it pays to use your M.I.N.D.

Dividends have represented 30-40% of total return. That is why investing in the ten highest dividend yielding stocks has beaten the Dow Jones Industrial Average dividend yield every year.

Past performance is no guarantee of future results.

BOND LADDERING

A great way to purchase bonds is to ladder them. To ladder bonds simply means to buy individual bonds with varying rates of maturity. As an illustration, if you planted an apple orchid and in the first acre you planted seedlings that would mature and produce seasoned apples in five years. On the second acre you planted small apple trees whose fruit would ripen into sweet edible apples in four years. Larger, more veteran trees are planted on the third acre and its apples would develop in three years. If you continued at this successive rate, the fifth acre would contain trees that had already produced ripe apples so that their fruit would be ready for market the very next year. As with laddering bonds, if the bonds have a sequential maturity rate, it reduces the overall risk and increases yield over time. It also takes the guesswork out of interest rates. This is a wonderful strategy; however, some people believe that bonds have no risk. There are several types of bond risks:

1.
Reinvestment risk

When you reinvest your matured bond capital, interest rates may have gone down. As a result, you have to reinvest at a lower rate. For example, you are holding a 6% coupon paying you $60 per bond a year. Once that bond matures, you might consider reinvestment. However, now interest rates have dropped so that the same type of bond is at a 5% coupon. At this point, you only receive $50 per bond a year. That is the risk involved when reinvesting.

2.
Interest rate risk

When interest rates go up, the value of bonds go down. Your bonds may fluctuate in value. If you decide to sell your bonds prior to maturity and the interest rates have gone up, you may have to sell them at a discount.

3.
Inflation and taxes

After you factor in inflation and taxes, most bonds just break even or even more devastating, they lose money. Remember, bonds are mainly purchased for preservation of wealth. In other words, you put your money into bonds because you want it back, not increased.

4.

Credit risk

You are relying on the companies' and countries' ability to pay back the principal and interest on the bond. This could create quite a risk. You may be familiar with some corporations that have gone into default and have been unable to pay interest on their bonds. This is referred to as ***trading flat***.

5.

Call risk

Some bond issuer reserve the right to buy back their bonds. If you have a 6% coupon paying $60 per bond each year, and interest rates go down to 4%, the company may call their bonds back. In other words, the bond issuer can buy back your bond before the maturity date. They then will give you the option to purchase the same bond with a lower interest rate. Your reissued bonds are now at 4% and subsequently, you will receive $40 a bond instead of $60. You stand to lose $20 per bond yearly. This is similar to refinancing your home. The company is refinancing their debt and paying a lower interest.

THE MILLIONAIRE-IN-TRAINING SOLUTION

The best way to reduce your bond risk and increase your overall yield is to ladder your bonds. Bonds with 10-year maturity dates pay more interest than bonds with 1-year maturity dates. Keep in mind, an interest payment is the amount of money you get in return for lending someone your money.

Every year, when your bonds mature you buy additional bonds with a 10-year maturity. If you run into a financial problem, you always have a bond nearing maturity. As I said previously, this strategy is a discipline. When a bond becomes due, purchase another bond, don't break the chain. You're on your way to becoming a millionaire, so remember to work on what you can control. Your **M**oney, **I**ntelligence, **N**eed and **D**iscipline.

The advantage of laddering is that it reduces reinvestment and interest rate risk because if interest rates go up, you will have a reserve to reinvest in new bonds; if interest rates go down, the bond you already have will go up.

STRATEGY TO BUILDING WEALTH

Some people believe that it takes a lot of money to obtain wealth. That simply is not true. It requires that you **use your money intelligently and you need to discipline yourself**. If I were to recommend the optimum strategy for building wealth, I would suggest dollar cost averaging. Dollar cost averaging is investing a predetermined amount into an investment monthly. Dollar cost averaging does not allow for reducing the monthly investment figure because the department store is having a red tag sale. This discipline requires that you invest the same amount each and every month.

Many investors say they are unable to maintain this discipline. They do not recognize that they are already dollar cost averaging. Our government mandates that you make duplicate percentage payments every time you receive your paycheck. The government is so determined to secure this payment that they automatically deduct their money before you even see your paycheck. They do this to be certain that a major portion of your taxes will be paid by the end of the year. What would happen if the government did not require this mandatory deduction? The IRS would have to change its name to the NRS, the Non-Revenue Service.

Dollar cost averaging is not difficult to maintain. It only requires a minimal amount of discipline. How many people have a monthly deduction with their Health Club? Or, how many of us have monthly magazine subscriptions that we do not read? Or worse yet, how many people spend monthly for lottery tickets and rarely, if ever, receive a return. It is amazing to me the number of people who refuse to invest monthly in their future. Dollar cost averaging is the ultimate wealth builder.

Dollar cost averaging can be especially successful during economic or political turmoil. Anti-millionaires did not invest, or, they stopped investing because of the significant events listed on page 81.

If you are already dollar cost averaging, you are right on target. Continue in your discipline. In dollar cost averaging we are comfortable in all market situations. The market can only go three ways: up, down, or sideways. If the market goes down, we are happy because we can buy quality companies at a discount. The stock market is the only place in the world where things go on sale and people panic. If the market stays the same, we are still sheltered because we are buying without incurring an increase in cost. If the market goes up, our investments have appreciated. We are buying fewer shares but our stock has increased in value.

Keep in mind, if the stock market went up every day, stocks would not be affordable for anyone. If ABC stock went up 10 points steadily each day, from $100 to $110; from $110 to $120 and so on, eventually you would not be in a position to purchase one tenth of a share. In which case, it is unreasonable to presume that the market will continue to climb daily. You cannot control the US stock market's day-to-day fluctuations but you can take advantage of it by investing monthly.

SIGNIFICANT MOMENTS IN HISTORY
THAT EFFECTED INVESTMENT

1934	The Depression	1967	Newark race riots
1935	Spanish civil war	1968	USS Pueblo seized
1936	Economy struggling	1969	Money tightens-market falls
1937	The Recession	1970	Cambodia invaded
1938	War clouds gather	1971	Wage price freeze
1939	War in Europe	1972	Largest US trade deficit
1940	France falls	1973	Energy crisis
1941	Pearl Harbor	1974	Steepest market drop in 40 years
1942	Wartime Price controls	1975	Clouded economic prospects
1943	Industry mobilize	1976	Economic recovery slows
1944	Consumer goods shortages	1977	Market slumps
1945	Postwar recession	1978	Interest rate rise
1946	DJA crosses 200-market too high	1979	Oil prices skyrocket
1947	Cold War begins	1980	Interest hit all-time high
1948	Berlin blockade	1981	Steep recession
1949	Russia explodes the A-bomb	1982	Worst recession in 40 years
1950	Korean War	1983	Market hits new highs
1951	Excessive profits tax	1984	Record federal deficits
1952	U.S seizes steel mills	1985	Economic growth slows
1953	Russia explodes A-bomb	1986	Dow nears 2000
1954	Dow crosses 300 market too high	1987	Record-setting market decline
1955	President Eisenhower's illness	1988	Election year
1956	Suez crisis	1989	October "mini crash"
1957	Russia launches Sputnik	1990	Persian Gulf crisis
1958	Recession	1991	Communism tumbles in Russia
1959	Castro seizes power in Cuba	1992	Global recession
1960	Russia downs U-2 plane	1993	Health care reform
1961	Berlin wall erected	1994	One of the worst years for bonds
1962	Cuban missile crisis	1995	Dow breaks 5000 market too high
1963	Kennedy assassinated	1996	1st Dem. Pres. re-election since FDR
1964	Golf of Tonkin	1997	Asian turmoil
1965	Civil rights marches	1998	Rumors of Presidential impeachment
1966	Vietnam War escalates	1999	Y2k

What if I suggest that you dollar cost average daily at the rate of $9.00 per day which typically is the average amount any one person might spend on food and entertainment. Let's look at what $9 can do: $9 each day times 7 days a week is $63. Multiply that $63 by the 4 weeks in a month and you will have accumulated $252. Round that off to $250 monthly. Imagine your investment savings if you squirreled away $250 each month. You are still using your M.I.N.D. and it is bringing you closer to becoming a millionaire.

```
: T.I₂₁ :CK₆₄ ER₄₄ :TIPS₈₇ :
```
Buy on weakness and sell on strength.

MFS, a rather large financial institution that created the first mutual fund in the United States called The Massachusetts Investors Trust, has an excellent illustration. The illustration displays the development of an investment initiated with $4,000 in December of 1972. The illustration depicts the growth when $250 is added on the last day of each month until April 30, 1999. This $250 per month (x12) equals $3,000 per year.

The benefits of dollar cost averaging and the discipline of investing monthly without waiver have now been evaluated. The two concepts that must be absorbed are: 1) investing without being influenced by outside events; and 2) your ability to manage a budget. People who can focus on their financial goal and delay gratification are millionaires in training.

When you go in and out of the stock market, you have to be right twice. When you buy a house, you don't call the bank everyday to check the value of the house. The house is a long-term investment with an assumed value. That is the mind-set you should have when you invest in securities.

Many people are buying mutual funds for all the wrong reasons. I want to empower you with the ability to look at mutual funds and evaluate their worth. First, call your financial advisor or the mutual fund company and ask for a prospectus. Also, inquire about the fund's top 10 holdings.

You should find a fund that has the same objective that you have for yourself. As an example, if you were saving for a retirement in 10 years, you should review growth funds. If you were only a few years away from retirement, review a more conservative fund.

When you evaluate the performance of a fund, don't just look at a few years. Look at how the fund has performed in a five to ten year period. This long-term view will tell you how the fund has performed in strong and weak markets.

The most important strategy in investing in mutual funds is to invest the same amount monthly; dollar cost averaging.

How would you invest $100,000? Stocks, mutual funds or perhaps a combination of both. Open a brokerage account, IRA or Roth IRA. You can combine several investment strategies. You can dollar cost average with a mutual fund into an IRA.

Two additional investment strategies are investing in a retirement or qualified plan. Many people do not take advantage of the investment opportunities offered by their employer. I always suggest investing in a 401k, 403b, SEP or IRA. To maximize its benefits, it would be advantageous to contribute as much as you can, regardless of what the company matches.

MFS MASS INVESTORS TRUST C
Hypothetical Table

Period End	Invest	Dividend Income	Capital Gains	Reinvest	Shares	NAV	Market Value
12/01/1972	4,000	0	0	0	296	13.51	4,000
12/31/1972	250	0	183	183	330	12.89	4,249
12/31/1973	3,000	184	88	272	617	10.74	6,629
12/31/1974	3,000	324	0	324	997	7.60	7,575
12/31/1975	3,000	429	224	653	1,382	9.57	13,224
12/31/1976	3,000	557	365	922	1,737	11.24	19,522
12/31/1977	3,000	803	324	1,127	2,154	9.43	20,315
12/31/1978	3,000	1,059	395	1,454	2,619	9.59	25,113
12/31/1979	3,000	1,428	994	2,422	3,136	10.83	33,967
12/31/1980	3,000	1,850	2,999	4,849	3,777	12.65	47,775
12/31/1981	3,000	2,285	3,508	5,793	4,550	10.63	48,364
12/31/1982	3,000	2,708	4,699	7,407	5,534	11.04	61,093
12/31/1983	3,000	2,676	7,492	10,168	6,632	11.61	76,998
12/31/1984	3,000	3,173	3,190	6,363	7,481	11.02	82,443
12/31/1985	3,000	3,578	8,680	12,259	8,752	12.12	106,074
12/31/1986	3,000	3,587	16,016	19,603	10,537	12.09	127,395
12/31/1987	3,000	4,247	15,170	19,417	12,396	11.26	139,577
12/31/1988	3,000	4,950	10,455	15,405	14,009	11.22	157,182
12/31/1989	3,000	6,481	17,849	24,330	16,040	13.55	217,338
12/31/1990	3,000	6,953	13,687	20,640	17,930	12.28	220,180
12/31/1991	3,000	7,069	25,047	32,116	20,507	13.87	284,437
12/31/1992	3,000	7,079	47,120	54,199	25,073	12.31	308,648
12/31/1993	3,000	9,851	42,801	52,652	29,803	11.50	342,734
12/31/1994	3,000	7,424	32,623	40,047	33,982	10.07	342,203
12/31/1995	3,000	16,004	28,569	44,573	37,792	12.71	480,338
12/31/1996	3,000	7,136	50,831	57,967	42,045	14.33	602,501
12/31/1997	3,000	6,385	52,035	58,420	45,735	17.30	791,207
12/31/1998	3,000	2,525	48,760	51,285	48,596	19.95	969,498
04/30/1999	1,000	363	4,914	5,277	48,910	20.53	1,004,130
Total	83,250	111,108	439,018	550,126			

Ending Amount Attributable to:	Market Value	Shares
Principal	141,982	6,916
Income	180,472	8,791
Capital Gains	681,676	33,204
Total Ending Amount:	**1,004,130**	**48,911**

Past performance is not a guarantee of future results. Please review prospectus before investing and consult a financial advisor. Initial and subsequent investments are not subject to sales charges. Taxes are assumed to come from another source. Capital gain and income dividends are reinvested.

State of California	Paycheck	MIT Paycheck
Gross Salary	$2500.00	$2500.00
Retirement Savings	$.00	$150.00
Taxable Salary	$2500.00	$2350.00
Social Security	$191.25	$191.25
Federal Tax	$321.75	$286.25
State Tax	$81.02	$69.02
Take Home Pay	$1905.98	$1803.48
Top Tax Bracket	36.00%	23.00%

In a retirement plan you have several benefits. First, it serves as a tax deduction. Second, there is tax deferred growth, which means as long as the money stays in the plan, you don't have to pay taxes on the capital gain or dividends. It is disciplined. The money is taken out before you get your check.

Planning for your future retirement is not as difficult as most people think. The following is the estimated monthly paycheck for an individual who makes $30,000 annually. In a review of the paycheck we learn the difference between investing in a retirement plan (MIT paycheck) versus not investing at all. The Millionaire In Training saves $150.00 each month towards her retirement plan.

First, examine the difference in the Take-Home pay. An individual who does not plan for the future takes home $1905.98. The Millionaire In Training takes home $1803.48, a difference of $102.50. However, while investing $150.00 in your future retirement, your tax savings is $47.50 or $570.00 annually. Therefore, if you do not invest in a retirement fund, you are giving Uncle Sam $570.00 every year. Is that something you could use?

I also have an example of an individual who makes $60,000 annually. This example is double the annual salary, but the paycheck difference between the MIT future investment planner and the individual who chose not to invest is $101.97. The tax savings are $68.04, which adds up to $816.48 yearly.

State of California	Paycheck	MIT Paycheck
Gross Salary	$5000.00	$5000.00
Retirement Savings	$.00	$170.00
Taxable Salary	$5000.00	$4830.00
Social Security	$382.50	$382.50
Federal Tax	$1026.38	$974.15
State Tax	$308.40	$292.59
Take Home Pay	$3282.72	$3180.76
Top Tax Bracket	40.30%	37.30%

These are only illustrations and DO NOT reflect available investment options. Any distribution is subject to ordinary income taxes upon receipt. Before-Tax savings are fully taxable upon receipt. How much your retirement savings will be worth depends on how much is contributed and your interest/investment earnings. The state taxes may vary from state to state.

If your company does not offer a retirement plan, open an Individual Retirement Account (IRA). Let us take a look at the power of investing in a simple IRA and the power of tax deferred growth. You will be amazed at the difference between the growth in an IRA and its tax-deferred potential as it compares to a taxable savings account. Our friend, Mil N. Aire, has $4000.00 per year to invest. At the beginning of year one, he puts $2000.00 into an IRA and $2000.00 into a taxable account, which yields 10%. Each year, he deposits $2000 into each investment. Imagine Mr. Aire's surprise upon retirement when he discovers that his IRA literally doubled his taxable account.

If you look at the difference of $500,000, no further illustration is necessary. The fundamental premise here is, 'Use your money wisely.'

Additionally, this illustration represents a relentless discipline. Without a doubt, over the years, Mr. Aire certainly had opportunities to spend his money on extravagant vacations, or a more expensive car, or pull his money out of the account anytime the stock market showed a decline. However, he continued to invest the same amount each year faithfully. He used his M.I.N.D (**M**oney, **I**ntelligence, **N**eed and **D**iscipline).

The same rules apply in a 401k and 403b or any other qualified plan. You can save up to $10,000 or 15% of income; whichever is less. If you are self-employed you can do a SEP (Simplified Employee Pension) in which you can save up to 24,000 or 15% of income; whichever is less.

Another option is a Roth IRA. This is similar to a traditional IRA in that you can save $2000 annually. The difference in a Roth IRA is that you are not entitled to the up-front deduction; however, upon retirement at age 59 ½ or above, the distributions are tax-free. You may have a better wealth accumulator at your fingertips if your job has a 401k 403b or SEP. Take advantage of this retirement benefit. I once had a woman explain to me that her company did not match the 401k employee contribution so she was not going to participate in the 401k plan. This was a very foolish strategy. Whether her employer contributed or not, she would still have nothing in 20 years if she did not participate. What is she going to do

> **MILLIONAIRE MOMENT**
>
> If you wish to give away money to your favorite Uncle Sam, then don't save in a retirement fund.

years from now when she is retired? Can she go into a grocery store and tell the store manager to lower the price of food because her company did not match the 401k benefits? Her view of investments is very narrow.

MIL N. AIRE'S SAVINGS

Year	IRA Account	Taxable Account
1	$ 2,209	$ 2,151
2	4,650	4,464
3	7,347	6,951
4	10,325	9,626
5	13,616	12,502
6	17,251	15,596
7	21,267	18,922
8	25,703	22,500
9	30,604	26,347
10	36,018	30,484
11	41,999	34,933
12	48,607	39,718
13	55,906	44,863
14	63,969	50,396
15	72,877	56,346
16	82,718	62,745
17	93,589	69,627
18	105,598	77,027
19	118,865	84,985
20	133,521	93,543
21	149,712	102,746
22	167,598	112,644
23	187,357	123,287
24	209,186	134,733
25	233,299	147,042
26	259,938	160,278
27	289,367	174,513
28	321,877	189,821
29	357,791	206,283
30	397,466	223,986
31	441,295	243,024
32	489,714	263,497
33	543,202	285,514
34	602,292	309,191
35	667,570	334,652
36	739,682	362,034
37	819,346	391,480
38	907,352	423,145
39	1,004,573	457,199

This graph is for illustrative purposes only.

COVERED CALL STRATEGY

I am going to reveal to you an ideal strategy for generating cash flow through the use of stocks. It is called covered call writing. Before we go over the advantages of this concept, let us understand the covered call strategy conceptually.

Remember our friend, Mil N. Aire? He paid $48,000.00 for an automobile. His neighbor, Market Maker Mike, offers him a deal. Mike said, "I would like to buy your car for $50,000 within the next three months and for that right, I will pay you $2,000." The two gentlemen agree. If we examine this transaction through millionaire vision, we learn that Mike is going to attempt to sell the car for more than $52,000 to make a quick profit.

> ### EXAMPLE
>
> For example, our buddy Mil has purchased 100 shares of a company at $28.00 a share. He uses the same strategy. He sells the *right* not the *obligation* to someone to take it from him at $30.00 a share within three months and he is compensated for this at $3.00 a share.

There are three things that can happen.

1) The car can appreciate in value to $55,000 and Mil makes $4,000 ($50,000 – $48,000 = 2000 + 2000 premium = 4000).

2) Mike makes $3000 (50,000 car + $2000 premium paid is $52,000; $55,000–$52,000 = $3,000).

3) On the other hand, the car can go down; Mil makes $2,000 and still has the car; or the price could stay the same and Mil still keeps the car and the $2,000; and yes, Mil can repeat the process after the 3 months is over.

Regardless of what happens, Mil keeps his $2,000 premium. He misses the home run hit. He will, as they say in baseball, just hit singles and doubles. He is giving up the home run hit. You can do the same strategy with stocks. You are renting stock to someone and you get paid for it.

Again, the stock can do three things: go up, down, or sideways. In all three scenarios, Mil gets to keep his $300 or premium in option terms. Let's say the stock goes to $35.00. How much does Mil get? Thirty dollars a share, which is $3,000 plus his $300 premium makes a $3,300 total. On the other hand, the stock goes down to $27 at expiration. Mil's value of $2,700 plus his $300 premium puts him at $3,000; not bad on a $2,800 dollar investment that went down. Or, let's just say the stock stayed at $28 and Mil keeps the $300 dollars. His total value is $3,100 and the process starts all over again. He can sell another contact. Covered call writing is just another way of creating income other than through dividends. The downside is that you cap your upside potential. You will only get the strike price, no more. Mil's advantage is that he gets paid for holding stock and reduces the risk of stock ownership. Technically, a call option gives the buyer the *right* not the *obligation* to purchase a security at a specific price by a certain period of time and pays a premium for that right. Don't get nervous when you hear the word *option* because I am going to show you a strategy to reduce risk, not add to it.

Options involve risk. Before investing, you need to review a pamphlet called Characteristics and Risks of Standardized Options. Simply call the *Chicago Board Options Exchange (CBOE) at (800) OPTIONS* to obtain this information. The CBOE also has an excellent website at *www.cboe.com*. Or, you can contact your financial advisor; who should have some pamphlets available.

Chapter

VI

The Game Plan

In the beginning of this book, I discussed the Millionaire-In-Training strategy, which primarily involves using your M.I.N.D. For those of you who find it necessary to turn the pages back for a review, I will save you the time.

MONEY, INTELLIGENCE, NEED AND DISCIPLINE.

In line with the four basic food groups, these elements are necessary to strengthen you financially. The challenge faced by most people is implementation of this discipline. How do you change financial directions when you have been going this way for so long? You have heard a variation of the age-old myth about men who will drive lost for hours because they do not want to ask for directions. As men, we know where we are going, it is the destination that is lost. It sounds funny, (especially to most women), but fundamentally the premise is the same. If you have been operating one way for so long, after a period of time, your mind set will not allow you to change directions or ask for help.

So, most people continue on the same route. There are six crucial habits that negatively affect your financial independence. If you find your course on any of these routes, it is time for you to turn around. Time to go in a new direction. Here are six habits that will obstruct your way to financial independence:

1. **Lack of direction**
   If you do not have a system or mechanism in place, then you will simply wander from idea to idea. We need to set goals that are specific, attainable and contain realistic timetables. Having no plan at all is planning to fail.

2. **Short-term focus**
   Making short-term decisions that have long term ramifications is a definite hindrance. Not investing because you want to save for your summer vacation or buying penny stock because it is cheap is what I call the "ruler mentality". If I asked you how far away you lived from your job, you would tell me in miles. If I handed you a ruler and asked you to tell me in inches, you might think that I was crazy. The same holds true for investments. You don't look at day-to-day market fluctuations; you set your focus on a long-term outlook. You have to look further than tomorrow or next week.

3. **Debt**
   If you are overcome with debt, you are still investing. It is called negative investing. The problem is you will be on your way to becoming an antimillioanire, that is to say you are making someone else rich.

4. **Lack of discipline**
   You have to have that need in M.I.N.D. Your need for financial independence has to be stronger than your desire to keep up with the Joneses. We have to stay properly allocated. If we have all quality stock and 5 go up and 1 goes down, we have to be disciplined enough not to sell the one that went down. We have to stick with the game plan.

5.   Making excuses

You can do two things, make excuses or make money. If you are reading this book carefully then your desire is to make money. So, get rid of the excuses.

6.   Listening to the wrong advice

My motto has always been, "Don't take advice from people more messed up than you". Sometimes we take advice from people that are deeper in debt than we are ourselves. If I hurt my arm, I go to a doctor, not to a co-worker. If my car breaks down, I go to a mechanic, not to a gardener. You would be surprised how many people get financial advice from people who really know very little about investing.

The game plan is complete if you have all points working *positively* in synergy. However, there are two very important points that standout. They are numbers 4, (lack of discipline) and 6, (listening to the wrong advice). When you do not have a grasp on those two points, it is tantamount to "losing your M.I.N.D.". They are the "I.D." to success. Intelligence (securing good advice) and **D**iscipline. Those two features will carry you through if you are weak in any of the other areas. First, let's examine your intelligence.

Securing sound financial advice should come from a professional. Many people ask themselves, do I need a financial advisor? I believe you do. A good relationship with a qualified investment professional can only enhance your results. First, a financial professional is someone who assists you in achieving your financial goals. Financial professionals use several different names such as Financial Planner, Financial Consultant and Stockbroker. It is not so much what they are called as much as what they do. Initially, a plan is developed towards achieving your goals. Most goals are savings, retirement, college planning or building wealth. Aspects of financial planning include:

1.   Cash management and budgeting
2.   Insurance
3.   Investment management
4.   Retirement planning
5.   Estate planning

The challenge is to locate the *right* Financial Planner. The best way to find one is through a referral. Ask friends, family or a neighborhood Pastor. Once you receive a referral, meet and talk to the prospective planner. Here are some questions you may want to ask:

1. Who are your typical clients?
2. What do you specialize in or what are your areas of expertise?
3. What type of investments do you use?
4. How are you compensated?

Some responses to look for are:

1. The typical client should have a profile similar to yours.
2. Your planner's area of expertise should coincide with your desired goals.
3. The explanation should be clear and concise. If the advisor does not take the time to explain investments to you clearly, time will show that he does not have the patience you will require
4. Planners are compensated in 3 ways:
   (a) Commission—when a security is bought or sold a commission is charged,
   (b) Fee only—a flat annual or hourly fee,
   (c) Fee base—compensation on a percentage of the money under management.

Working on *commission*, the professional is paid to buy and sell stock. Money is made through buying and selling, not from investment performance. The challenge with a *fee only* arrangement is that an hourly charge will most times discourage clients from seeking advice when they should. With a *fee-based* compensation, you are on the same side of the table. The only way for the planner to make more money is to grow your assets. The planner has to work smarter for the money.

Once you have decided on a planner, ask yourself these six questions:

1. Do I feel comfortable with this planner?
2. Does the planner have my best interest in mind?
3. Does the planner respect my feelings and insecurities about money?
4. Will this person educate me about investments?
5. Do I feel comfortable talking to this person? Are we compatible?
6. Is this person competent, honest, ethical and trustworthy?

If these elements are in place, check the credentials of the person and his/her firm. Make sure the advisor is registered to do business in your state. After this, you have found your trusted advisor. You are now operating with **Intelligence**.

Now, let us take a closer look at your **Discipline**. Without it, you cannot hope to succeed. You have to stay the course. Let me show you how discipline works. Let's suppose you have been investing for several years. Suddenly, you decide to stop investing for approximately five years. The Hypothetical illustration on the following page is an example through a mutual fund from Alliance Capital. My friends, Nick Willet and Jeff Kuster of Alliance Capital were nice enough to send me this information. It will illustrate an initial investment of $4,000.00 and then $250.00 paid monthly ($3,000.00/year). You will note in Hypothetical Illustration I that the individual

ALLIANCE GROWTH & INCOME A

Reinvest Income Yes		Reinvest CapGains Yes	Load Fee 4.25%		Redemption Fee None	12b-1 Fee 0.25%	

Period Ends	Capital Invest	Market Income	Gains	Reinvest	Value	NAV	Shares
12/31/71	4,000	0	0	0	3,828	3.78	1,013
12/31/72	3,000	148	238	386	7,548	4.10	1,841
12/31/73	3,000	251	344	595	9,169	3.28	2,795
12/31/74	3,000	410	399	810	9,786	2.32	4,218
12/31/75	3,000	595	511	1,106	16,335	2.89	5,652
12/31/76	3,000	735	775	1,510	23,028	3.28	7,021
12/31/77	3,000	905	950	1,854	23,939	2.77	8,642
12/31/78	3,000	1,111	1,259	2,370	28,035	2.65	10,579
12/31/79	3,000	1,519	1,630	3,150	34,355	2.69	12,771
12/31/80	3,000	2,167	2,100	4,267	45,568	2.97	15,343
12/31/81	3,000	2,577	2,818	5,395	48,235	2.62	18,410
12/31/82	3,000	3,038	3,448	6,486	64,373	2.94	21,895
12/31/83	3,000	2,706	5,332	8,038	80,852	3.20	25,266
12/31/84	3,000	3,386	8,282	11,668	89,587	2.97	30,164
12/31/85	3,000	4,029	11,091	15,119	120,858	3.35	36,077
12/31/86	3,000	4,607	15,018	19,625	149,920	3.53	42,470
12/31/87	3,000	6,078	34,827	40,905	153,814	2.65	58,043
12/31/88	3,000	4,969	28,790	33,759	182,644	2.52	72,478
12/31/89	3,000	7,467	32,188	39,655	232,449	2.62	88,721
12/31/90	3,000	9,270	27,185	36,455	231,468	2.17	106,667
12/31/91	3,000	7,695	16,147	23,842	297,371	2.52	118,005
12/31/92	3,000	7,305	19,404	26,708	313,856	2.41	130,231
12/31/93	3,000	7,922	24,529	32,451	348,157	2.40	145,066
12/31/94	3,000	7,715	17,313	25,028	336,415	2.13	157,941
12/31/95	3,000	7,992	33,411	41,402	467,165	2.67	174,968
12/31/96	3,000	8,834	67,538	76,372	583,228	2.88	202,510
12/31/97	3,000	10,210	93,781	103,991	754,816	3.19	236,619
12/31/98	3,000	9,525	84,073	93,598	918,394	3.45	266,201
12/31/99	3,000	10,709	46,288	56,997	1,020,466	3.60	283,463
TOTAL	88,000	133,875	579,669	713,544			

Ending Amount Attributable to	Market Value	Shares
Principal:	103,787	28,830
Income:	171,276	47,577
Capital Gains:	745,403	207,056
Total Ending Amount:	1,020,466	283,463

Hypothetical Illustration I

ALLIANCE GROWTH & INCOME A

	Reinvest Income Yes	Reinvest CapGains Yes	Load Fee 4.25%		Redemption Fee None	12b-1 Fee 0.25%	
Period Ends	Capital Invest	Market Income	Gains	Reinvest	Value	NAV	Shares
12/31/71	4,000	0	0	0	3,828	3.78	1,013
12/31/72	3,000	148	238	386	7,548	4.10	1,841
12/31/73	0	214	263	477	6,470	3.28	1,973
12/31/74	0	250	222	473	5,056	2.32	2,179
12/31/75	0	277	224	501	6,839	2.89	2,366
12/31/76	0	288	291	579	8,362	3.28	2,549
12/31/77	0	310	313	624	7,662	2.77	2,766
12/31/78	3,000	394	473	867	11,000	2.65	4,151
12/31/79	3,000	636	706	1,342	15,289	2.69	5,684
12/31/80	3,000	1,009	1,000	2,009	22,084	2.97	7,436
12/31/81	3,000	1,288	1,432	2,720	24,864	2.62	9,490
12/31/82	3,000	1,606	1,849	3,455	34,860	2.94	11,857
12/31/83	3,000	1,484	2,957	4,441	45,167	3.20	14,115
12/31/84	3,000	1,913	4,723	6,637	51,404	2.97	17,308
12/31/85	3,000	2,331	6,462	8,794	70,730	3.35	21,114
12/31/86	3,000	2,711	8,882	11,594	88,856	3.53	25,200
12/31/87	3,000	3,625	20,881	24,506	92,315	2.65	34,836
12/31/88	3,000	3,001	17,440	20,442	110,834	2.52	43,982
12/31/89	3,000	4,556	19,676	24,233	142,284	2.62	54,307
12/31/90	3,000	5,703	16,753	22,456	142,831	2.17	65,821
12/31/91	3,000	4,765	10,024	14,789	184,710	2.52	73,298
12/31/92	3,000	4,552	12,117	16,669	196,081	2.41	81,361
12/31/93	3,000	4,963	15,397	20,360	218,626	2.40	91,094
12/31/94	3,000	4,857	10,921	15,777	212,288	2.13	99,666
12/31/95	3,000	5,055	21,165	26,220	296,029	2.67	110,872
12/31/96	3,000	5,608	42,926	48,534	370,778	2.88	128,742
12/31/97	3,000	6,500	59,756	66,256	481,044	3.19	150,798
12/31/98	3,000	6,077	53,681	59,758	586,487	3.45	169,996
12/31/99	3,000	6,845	29,605	36,450	652,757	3.60	181,321
TOTAL	73,000	80,968	360,379	441,346			

Ending Amount Attributable to	Market Value	Shares
Principal:	86,401	24,000
Income:	103,558	28,766
Capital Gains:	462,798	128,555
Total Ending Amount:	652,757	181,321

Hypothetical Illustration II

was disciplined. He invested monthly for a total of $3,000.00 each year and after 30 years of disciplined investing, the portfolio has grown to **One Million Dollars**.

However, in Hypothetical Illustration II, the individual started out with the same intentions but from 1973 to 1977 failed to remain disciplined and did not invest at all. The individual lost focus and as a result lost a considerable amount of money as well.

THE GROWTH OF A $10,000 INVESTMENT WHEN DIVIDENDS ARE REINVESTED

Years	4%	6%	8%	10%	12%
1	$10,000	$10,000	$10,000	$10,000	$10,000
2					
3					
4					
5					
6					$20,000
7				$20,000	
8					
9			$20,000		
10					
11					
12		$20,000			$40,000
13					
14				$40,000	
15					
16					
17					
18	$20,000		$40,000		$80,000
19					
20					
21				$80,000	
22					
23					
24		$40,000			$160,000
25					
26					
27			$80,000		
28				$160,000	
29					
30					$320,000
31					
32					
33					
34					
35					
36	$40,000	$80,000	$160,000	$320,000	$640,000

INVESTMENT DOUBLES EVERY....

18 Years	12 Years	9 Years	7 Years	6 Years

Hypothetical Illustration II shows that it cost this individual more than $350,000. The person did not think long term; the outcome was phenomenal lost revenue. Long-term thinking is not only sensible but its results are rewarding.

While reviewing the long-term investment, be sure to Intelligently pursue the investment that coincides with your goals. Take a look at the example on page 100.

This example shows how a $10,000 investment grows at various hypothetical rates of return when you reinvest dividends. As time passes, compounding begins to pay off and your investment grows. The higher your rate of return, the greater effect compounding has on your original investment. Compounding is interest on top of interest. Although, the stock market does fluctuate and cannot be guaranteed, we have to be astute when choosing the right investments. Investments in low interest bearing securities will certainly test your patience and many times undermine your efforts to **discipline yourself**. There is a rule in investing called "rule 72".

"Rule 72" allows you to determine how many years it will take for your investment to double through dividing 72 by the annual rate of return. For example, at an 8% annual growth rate, your investment doubles every 9 years (72÷8 = 9).

My advice is simple...maintain your **I.D.** if you plan to be a Millionaire In Training.

ACTION PLAN

This book is designed for you to build wealth and become financially independent. Like everything else in life, you will get out of this what you put into it. Now that you have educated yourself in the area of finances, let's put together a game plan for building wealth. We will start by reviewing your current net worth. Fill in the Net Worth Worksheet on the following page to gain an accurate look at your present financial condition. No one else will see it, so go ahead and put down factual information.

What would it take to double your cash flow or even better, add a 0 to it? If you make $50,000 annually, what would it take to raise your income to $500,000? Becoming a millionaire starts in the mind. Set your mind on increasing your wealth. Could you get a raise on your job or would you have to open a business? Expand your current business? Then, take the next step. What education would you need to get that amount of money? What would it take to grow your business? Have you attempted to contact the Small Business Administration in your city for the funds to expand your business? Who would you need to know to raise the level of your business or finances?

What would you have to do to increase your wealth? Start doing those things now.

NET WORTH WORKSHEET

Assets		Liabilities	
Cash	_____	Mortgage Payment	_____
Checking	_____	Home Equity Loan	_____
Savings/Money Market	_____	Car Loans	_____
Certificates of Deposit CD	_____	Credit Card Debt	_____
Mutual Funds	_____	Student Loans	_____
Stocks	_____	Loan Against 401k	_____
Bonds	_____	Margin	_____
Government Securities	_____	Taxes Owed	_____
Options	_____	Other	_____
Personal	_____		
Home	_____	Total Liabilities (B)	_____
Rental Property	_____		
Clothes	_____		
Home Furnishings	_____		
Art/Collectibles	_____		
Jewelry	_____		
Other	_____		

Net Worth (A – B) _____
(Total Assets minus Total Liabilities)

Total Assets (A) _____

After completing this worksheet, you now have an account of your current net worth. Do not get discouraged if it is not a million dollars because things are going to change. Remember that you are a Millionaire-In-Training!

INCOME WORKSHEET

Now that we know our net worth, let's find out where the money is coming from.

Monthly Income

Take Home Pay _____

2nd Job (hint, hint) _____

Commissions/Bonuses (after taxes) _____

Alimony _____

Child Support _____

Rents Collected from Income Property _____

Pensions and/or Social Security Income _____

Tax Returns _____

Other Outside Income _____

Total Income _____

SEND IN THE PLAY

We now know how much we have and where it all came from, so let's send in the play. With all of your preparation and all of your financial knowledge, you are going to start performing at an optimum level. How? By putting your financial plan into action.

1   When are you going to be completely debt free? Pick a date. Have a goal to work toward. Let us say *Feb 8, 2010.* (This timetable should include all debt, even your house.)

2   How much are you going to invest monthly? Determine an amount. A figure you can stick to without wavering. Once you have set this amount, do not decrease it for any reason. Continue to invest that amount through holidays, illness, family emergencies, layoffs, etc. You remember the drill.

3   Do you have a Personal Financial Statement — I, *Mil N. Aire,* will save $250 monthly and pay $850 toward the reduction of debt until February 2, 2010. After which, I will increase my monthly saving investment amount and pay cash for luxury items. When I retire in 12 years I will live in a 5-bedroom home in Beverly Hills, California with a guesthouse and pool. I will own a Lexus, BMW and Mercedes. I will give $50,000 a year to my church, synagogue or favorite charity. I will play golf 3 times a week. I will delay gratification and make a deposit into my future by saving 15% of my gross earnings towards investing. After paying off debt, I will move that savings amount up from 15% to 25 %. **I am now a Millionaire-In-Training!**

GLOSSARY OF TERMS

401k
> A company sponsored retirement plan in which you have the ability to contribute your income in a tax-deferred manner.

403b
> A retirement savings plan that is funded by employee contributions and (often) matching contributions from the employer. The employer is usually public school systems and other tax-exempt organizations. They can only invest in annuities or mutual funds.

Accrued Interest
> Interest that has accumulated between the last interest payment and the purchase date of a bond.

Aggressive Growth Fund
> Stock in a company that is small but rapidly expanding, giving the investor the opportunity to reach above-average returns.

Amortization
> The systematic reduction of a financial obligation, such as a mortgage.

Annual Report
> A document the stockholder receives once a year that includes the status of the invested in company. It contains the balance sheet, income statement and cash flows as well as discussions about business operations.

Annuitize
> The time or process in which an annuity holder elects to begin his payout of income. Once the annuitant elects to begin this payout, he must select the settlement option in which he desires to receive payments. At this time, all control of the owner contract is surrendered to the insurance company. When you annuitize a contract, you receive a payment for the rest of your life.

Annuity
> Form of contract sold by life insurance companies that guarantees a fixed or variable payment to the annuitant at some future time, usually retirement.

Appreciate
> To increase in value. (Very important for all Millionaires-in-Training.)

Ask Price
> The price you have to pay to purchase securities or mutual funds.

Asset Allocation
> Investing in a mix of stocks, bonds and cash to diversify and reduce risk.

At-The-Money
> An option is at-the-money if the underlying security is selling for the same price as the exercise price of the option.

Automatic Reinvestment

The option available to mutual fund shareholders whereby fund income dividends and capital gains distributions are automatically put back into the fund to buy new shares and thereby build up holdings. Stocks also have dividend reinvestment options.

Balance Sheet

Financial report also called 'Statement of Condition' or 'Statement of Financial Position'. The sheet displays the status of a company's assets, liabilities and the owner's equity on a given date. It is usually calculated at the end of the month.

Balanced Investments

Blending one or more of the investment categories. For example, your money could be in stocks, bonds, and money market funds. The different investments carry different levels of risk.

Bankruptcy

The condition in which corporations or individuals legally declare that they cannot meet their financial obligations.

Bear Market

A declining stock market.

Beneficiary

The person named in a policy to receive money or property after the death of the policyholder.

Bid

The highest price a prospective buyer is prepared to pay at a given time.

Blue-Chip Stock

Stock in a high quality company that has been in business for decades with long records of increased earnings and dividends.

Bond

A debt instrument issued by a company or government body to finance a certain aspect of its operation. When you buy bonds, you are lending money to the institution issuing the bond and you are entitled to receive interest on that loan.

Bond Fund

A mutual fund that invests in bonds.

Budget

A systematic plan of spending and saving your income over a definite period of time based on your income and expenses.

Bull Market

A rising stock market. (This is a good thing.)

Call Option

The right to buy a stated number of shares or other units of an underlying security at the exercise price within a stated period of time.

Capital Gains

The difference between an asset's purchase price and selling price, when the difference is positive.

Cash Value Insurance

Life insurance that combines a death benefit with a potential tax-deferred buildup of money (called cash value) in the policy.

Certificate of Deposit (CD)

A debt instrument issued by a bank that usually pays interest. Institutional CDs are issued in denominations of $100,000 or more and individual CDs start as low as $100. Maturities range from a few weeks to several years.

Collateral

The assets put up by a borrower as a pledge for a loan. The lender can take control of the collateral if the loan is not repaid.

Common Stock

A type of stock that entitles the owner to voting rights in a corporation. If the company goes out of business, it also entitles the holder to a claim on what remains after all the creditors and preferred stockholders have been paid.

Common Stock Fund

A mutual fund whose portfolio consists primarily of common stocks with an emphasis on growth.

Compound Interest

When a bank pays interest on both the principal and the interest in savings accounts. Also known as interest paid on interest.

Corporate Bond

Debt instruments issued by corporations as a means of raising money.

Coupon Bond

Bond issued with detachable coupons that must be presented to a paying agent or the issuer for semiannual interest payment. These are bearer bonds, so whoever presents the coupon is entitled to the interest.

Covered Call Writer

A seller of a call option who owns the underlying security upon which the option is written. A call writer is also considered to be covered if he holds, on a share-for-share basis, a call of the same class as the call written where the exercise price of the call held is equal to or less than the exercise price of the call written.

Credit

Your power to borrow money based on your reputation for repayment, your net income and your assets.

Creditor

An individual or institution to whom money is owed.

Custodian

A brokerage, bank or trust company with certain qualifications that hold in safekeeping monies and securities owned by an investment company or person. Mutual funds and retirement accounts also have custodians.

Debt

Money, goods, or services that one party is obligated to pay to another in accordance with an expressed or implied agreement. Debt may or may not be secured.

Default

Failure of a debtor to make timely payments of interest and principal as they come due.

Defensive Stock

A stock that has a steady stream of income earnings regardless of economic conditions. Some examples are food, drugs and utilities.

Depreciation

Loss of value.

Discretionary Income

The money you can spend as you please <u>after</u> you have paid bills, living expenses and **invested at least 10%** of your income.

Diversification

An investment strategy that relies upon distribution of investments among a variety of securities to minimize risk.

Dividend

A payment issued by a company that distributes part of its profits and earnings to shareholders.

Dollar Cost Averaging

Investing equal amounts of money at regular intervals regardless of whether the stock market is moving upward or downward. This reduces average share costs by automatically acquiring more shares in periods of lower securities' prices and fewer shares in periods of higher prices. This does not assure a profit or protect against depreciation in declining markets.

Dow Jones Industrial Average

Thirty actively traded Blue-chip stocks primarily industrial and service oriented household names such as American Express, Citigroup, Disney, Coke and General Electric.

Earning Per Share

A portion of a company's profit allocated to each outstanding share of common stock.

Equity

The ownership of securities.

Exercise Price

The price per unit at which the holder of an option may purchase (in case of a call option) or sell (in case of a put option), the indicated underlying security. It is also known as the striking price.

Expiration Date

The final date on which an option may be exercised is referred to as the 'expiration date'. The Saturday after the third Friday in an expiration month is the final date on which equity options, index options, and most debt options can be exercised. After the expiration date, the option is worthless.

Face Value

The sum stated on the face of a policy or note to be paid at maturity.

Fear and Greed Factor

An emotional response an investor will have solely based upon the rising and falling of stock prices. When the market goes up, people tend to get greedy and buy more stock. On the other hand, when the market goes down, people tend to become fearful and refuse to buy stock. A successful investor must learn to do the opposite.

Federal Deposit Insurance Corporation (FDIC)

A federal agency that insures deposits up to $100,000 at commercial banks.

Federal Insurance Contributions Act (FICA)

A plan to fund social security that allows the federal government to take funds out of your paycheck.

Financial Planner

A professional who provides advice identifying financial goals and the strategies available to meet those goals.

Fraud

Deception for personal gain by means of false statements.

Growth Funds

A mutual fund that invests in companies that have the potential to grow quickly or have explosive earnings. They will usually pay low or no dividends and the value of the stock has the potential to rise or fall quickly.

Growth Stock

A stock that has the potential of increasing its price as the company expands and prospers.

Income Fund

A mutual fund that invests in older, well-established companies. This type of fund grows slowly and pays relatively large dividends.

Index Option

Calls and puts on indexes of stocks. These options are traded on the New York, American, and Chicago Board Options Exchanges, among others. Broad-based indexes cover a wide range of companies and industries, whereas narrow-based indexes consist of stocks in one industry or sector of the economy.

Individual Retirement Account (IRA)

Employed people can make annual contributions of up to $2,000 into this tax-deferred account. The owner of the account may make withdrawals from the account without penalty after the age of 59 ½.

Inflation

The rate at which the real cost of goods and services rises in the economy. The average rate of inflation according to the U.S Department of Labor is about 5.4%.

Initial Public Offering (IPO)

A corporation's first offering of stock to the public. IPOs are invariably an opportunity for the existing investors and participating venture capitalist to make huge profits since, for the first time, their shares will be given a market value reflecting expectations for the company's future growth.

Interest

Payment on money that is borrowed above the actual amount borrowed.

Intrinsic Value

A value compared to the prevailing market prices people are willing to pay. The person or people rather than the actual cost of the item or service usually determine the value.

Investment

The money you put into some form of property or security for income or profit, such as a home or pension plan.

Investment Grade

A bond with a rating of AAA to BBB.

Investment Objective

The goals that an investor sets for a portfolio.

Investment Return

The amount of value your investment gains or loses over a given period of time.

Junk Bond

Sometimes called high yield bond, a bond graded less than BBB. Because it is rated so low by the bond rating companies, it produces a higher yield. It is a higher risk and receives a higher return than an investment grade corporate bond.

Laddered Portfolio

When you build a laddered portfolio, you spread the dollar amount of your investment among securities with different maturity dates.

Liability

An obligation to pay a certain amount to another party.

Lien

A creditor's legal right to sell the mortgaged assets of a debtor when the debtor fails to meet loan payments.

Liquidity

The ability to buy or sell an asset quickly and in large volume without substantially affecting the asset's price.

Load

Sales charge paid by the investor who buys shares in a mutual fund or annuity.

Market Risk

The risk that the stock market will decline.

Maturity

The time period of a loan.

Money Market Fund

A mutual fund that invests in short-term, low risk, usually commercial paper, CD and Treasury Bills all of which mature within 12 months.

Mortgage

A debt instrument by which the borrower gives the lender a lien on property as security for the repayment of a loan. The borrower has use of the property, and the lien is removed when the obligation is fully paid. A mortgage normally involves real estate.

Municipal Bond

Debt security issued by cities that is free of federal taxes and may be exempt from state taxes if the purchaser lives in the state in which the issuing municipality is located.

Mutual Fund

An investment company that pools the resources of hundreds or thousands of individuals to enable them to diversify in a variety of investments, including stocks, bonds and money markets.

Net Asset Value (NAV)

In mutual funds, the market value of a fund share, synonymous with bid price. In the case of no-load funds, the NAV, market price, and offering price are all the same figure.

Net Income

The money available to you after all taxes have been subtracted from your gross income.

New York Stock Exchange (NYSE)

The largest and most active stock market in the world.

Option

In general it is a right to buy or sell property that is granted in exchange for an agreed upon sum. If the right is not exercised after a specified period, the option expires and the option buyer forfeits the money.

Owner's Equity

Paid-in Capital, donated capital, and retained earnings less the liabilities of a corporation.

Par

Equal to the nominal or Face value of a security. A bond selling at par, for instance, is worth the same dollar amount it was issued for or at which it will be redeemed at maturity — typically, $1000 per bond.

Par Value

With common stock, par value is set by the company issuing the stock. It is an assigned amount used to compute the dollar accounting value of the common shares on a company's balance sheet.

Penny Stock

A stock whose cost is less than $5.00. It is usually issued for new business ventures. The potential for fraud is high because the underlying companies are unknown and possibly unstable. They are usually thinly traded and not followed with much research.

Pension Plan

An arrangement that allows an employer to pay retirement benefits to employees.

Ponzi Scheme

An investment fraud named after Charles A. Ponzi who ran a large scam in the 1920s. It works on a pyramid principle whereby early investors are paid off with money coming from succeeding waves of investors who lure more investors, the last of whom lose the most.

Portfolio

A group of investments.

Preferred Stock

Class capital stock that pays dividends at a specified rate and that has preference over common stock in the payment of dividends and the liquidation of assets. Preferred stock does not ordinarily carry voting rights.

Prospectus

A detailed brochure explaining the investment objectives, type of investments, management style, fees, risks and other information concerning a mutual fund or other investment.

Put Option

With **Bonds:** bondholder's right to redeem a bond before maturity. With Options: a contract that grants the right to sell at a specified price a specific number of shares by a certain date. The put option buyer gains this right in return for payment of an option premium. The put option seller grants the right in return for receiving the premium.

Rate of Return

A measure of the income that an investment will yield.

Rider

An endorsement that changes the terms of an existing insurance policy.

Risk

The potential for the value or return on an investment to drop or become less than expected.

Securities and Exchange Commission SEC

A federal regulatory agency that oversees and administers the securities laws.

Security

> In Finance: Collateral offered by a debtor to a lender to secure a loan called collateral security.
>
> In **Investing:** an instrument that signifies an ownership position in a corporation (a stock), a creditor relationship with a corporation or governmental body (a bond), or rights to ownership such as those represented by an option.

Share

> A single unit of ownership in a corporation or mutual fund.

Shareholder

> A person who owns stock in a corporation or mutual fund.

Simplified Employee Pension (SEP)

> A pension plan in which both the employee and the employer contribute to an individual retirement account.

Speculation

> Taking on higher risk in anticipation of a higher return but understanding the higher than average possibility of loss.

Stock

> A share of ownership in a corporation.

Stock Market

> A place where people buy and sell shares of corporate ownership.

Strike Price

> The price at which the stock or commodity underlying a call or put option can be purchased (call) or sold (put) over the specified period.

Tax Bracket

> A designation that determines what percentage of income must be paid in taxes. Theoretically, the more income an individual receives, the higher the tax bracket, and the larger the percentage of taxes owed.

Tax Shelter

> An investment used for deferring, eliminating, or reducing income taxes.

Tax-deferred Account

> An account that contains funds that are not taxed until a later date.

Term Insurance

> A policy payable at death if that event occurs during the specified term or length of the insurance policy. An insurance contract that has no cash value.

Total Return

> All the money you made in an investment. Total return is the difference between the original purchase price of an investment and the current value of the shares plus all dividends and interest received.

U.S. Savings Bond

> A security issued by the U.S Treasury. The interest is exempt from state and local taxes and it usually matures from 10 to 30 years.

U.S. Treasury Note

> Intermediate-term debt security of the U.S Treasury. It matures from 2 to 10 years.

U.S. Treasury Bill

> A short-term debt security of the U.S Treasury. It usually matures in a year or less.

Unearned Income

Income such as dividends, interest payments or other income that is not received as a salary or wages.

Volatility

The amount a security moves up or down over a short period of time.

Yield

Generally, the return on an investment in a stock or bond, calculated at a percentage of the amount invested.

Zero-coupon Bond

A bond issued at a discount that increases in value as it approaches maturity but provides no periodic interest payment.

BONUS INFORMATION

Here is bonus information about getting your credit report back on track. The first thing you should do is obtain a copy of all three credit reports. It is useless to clean up just one report and leave the others.

EXPERIAN
Consumer Assistance
P.O. Box 2104
Allen, TX 75013
(888) 397-3742
www.experian.com

TRANSUNION
Consumer Assistance
P.O. Box 390
Springfield, PA 19064
(800) 916-8800
www.transunion.com

EQUIFAX
Credit Information Services
P.O. Box 105873
Atlanta, GA 30348
(800) 685-1111
www.equifax.com

CREDIT SCORES: WHAT DO THEY MEAN?

Your credit score is a key factor in determining your access to credit and the interest rate you will be charged. The list of users for credit scores is growing. Auto and homeowners-insurance companies are looking at credit scores to gauge customers future claims and setting premiums. Employees are screening job aplicants and landlords consult them before renting.

You can either call or write the credit agencies. They will charge between $8-$10 for your credit reports unless you have been refused credit in the last 30 days. If you have been refused credit in the last 30 days, then the agency will send the report at no cost to you. Also, Experian, formerly TRW, provides one complimentary copy a year.

I advise that you clear up *everything* on your credit reports. If your name is common, like mine, you may have several errors. If you have errors, write to the creditor with a copy of your last statement and inform them of the erroneous information that is damaging to your credit report. Ask them to please send you all information regarding your account or have it removed (*sample letter on next page*). Thank them in advance for their cooperation.

ACTION PLAN TO CLEAN UP CREDIT REPORT

1. Obtain credit reports from credit bureaus.
2. Find out what is inaccurate on the reports.
3. Write letters of verification. Follow up with credit reporting agencies.
4. You are done. Start thinking about making **MONEY**.